THE MONOPOLIES AND MERGERS COMMISSION

British Airports Authority

A Report on the efficiency and costs of, and the
service provided by, the British Airports Authority
in its commercial activities

Presented to Parliament by the Secretary of State for Trade and Industry
by Command of Her Majesty
December 1985

LONDON
HER MAJESTY'S STATIONERY OFFICE
£9·25 net

Cmnd. 9644

ISBN 0 10 196440 4

Members of the Monopolies and Mergers Commission as at 2 September 1985

Sir Godfray Le Quesne QC* *(Chairman)*
Mr H H Hunt *(Deputy Chairman)*
Sir Alan Neale KCB MBE *(Deputy Chairman)*
Mr D G Richards *(Deputy Chairman)*
Mr J G Ackers
Mr C C Baillieu
Mr M B Bunting
Mr K S Carmichael CBE
Sir Robert Clayton CBE
Mr P H Dean
Professor K D George*
Mr H L G Gibson OBE
Professor R M Goode OBE
Mr D G Goyder
Mr G D Gwilt
Mr L Kelly
Mr M S Lipworth
Professor S C Littlechild
Miss P K R Mann*
Mr S McDowall CBE
Mr L A Mills
Mr B C Owens*
Professor R Rees
Mr J S Sadler CBE*
Mr N L Salmon
Mr R G Smethurst
Sir Ronald Swayne MC
Mr D P Thomson*
Mr C A Unwin MBE
Mr S Wainwright CBE
 Mr N E D Burton *(Secretary)*

---

*These members formed the Group which was responsible for this report (see paragraph 2.3).

Note by the Department of Trade and Industry

In accordance with sections 17(4) and 17(5) of the Competition Act 1980, the Secretary of State for Trade and Industry has excluded from the copies of the report as laid before Parliament, and as published, certain matters publication of which appears to the Secretary of State to be against the public interest or which are matters relating to the affairs of particular persons whose interests would, in his opinion, be seriously and prejudicially affected by publication and publication of which appears to him not to be in the public interest. Accordingly certain parts of six tables and one figure and certain figures in the text have been omitted. The omissions are indicated by a note in square brackets.

No exclusions have been made from Chapter 14, Overall assessment: the public interest: summary of conclusions: the future.

Contents

Chapter   *Page*

	Glossary ..	vii
1	Summary ..	1
2	Introduction	17
3	The British Airports Authority ..	20
4	BAA commercial activities	26
5	BAA organisation and planning	43
6	Information and computing	55
7	Financial framework	63
8	Capital expenditure	75
9	Concessions and licences	82
10	Rents and property	89
11	Competition	97
12	Manpower efficiency and industrial relations ..	112
13	Quality of service	117
14	Overall assessment: the public interest: summary of conclusions: the future	126

Appendices

The numbering of appendices indicates the chapters to which they relate.

2.1	Interested third parties ..	136
3.1	BAA airports compared with some other major airports	138
3.2	British Airports Authority: organisation chart	139
3.3	Organisation chart showing responsibilities of Commercial Development Director ..	140
5.1	Extract from 1985 Corporate Plan (policy section) ..	141
5.2	Extract from 1985 Corporate Plan (strategy section) ..	143
5.3	BAA Corporate Plan—arrangements for its preparation	146
5.4	The development of airport commercial functions between 1983 and 1985 ..	150
6.1	Property management ..	152
6.2	Current trading information systems ..	155
7.1	BAA: budgets, out-turn and variances	156
7.2	BAA: commercial contributions to non-controllable costs and profits ..	157
7.3	Commercial activities: current cost income and expenditure by airport ..	158
7.4	Commercial activities: CCA return on capital employed	165
12.1	BAA manpower plan ..	166
12.2	Pay for non-industrial employees	167
12.3	Joint negotiating and consultative machinery ..	168
12.4	Heathrow airport negotiating and consultative machinery	169
13.1	Summary of passenger service standards	170

Glossary

Airside

Refers to that area of an airport accessible only to those specially authorised (for example, passengers with boarding cards, airline and airport operational staff).

ATM

Air transport movement—a landing or a take-off by aircraft operating a scheduled or non-scheduled service.

ATS

Air traffic services—a generic term applying to flight information, alerting service, air traffic advisory service, air traffic control service, area control service, approach control service, and aerodrome control service.

Commercial

Used in two senses in our report:
(1) to define those BAA activities which are the subject of our terms of reference—see paragraph 2.1;
(2) to define those commercial activities (as defined in our terms of reference) which are the primary responsibility of airport managements—see paragraph 5.37.

In most cases the context will make clear the sense in which the word is used. See also Trading.

Grandfather rights

Those rights to provide ground handling services which certain airlines have held for many years (in some cases since before the Authority's inception) at Heathrow.

Landside

Refers to that area of an airport open to the public generally.

Rack rent

A rent representing the full annual value (or very nearly) of the property.

Scheduled service

A service publicly advertised by an airline through its issued timetables. Non-scheduled services are other flights by airlines carrying passengers or cargo, eg charter flights.

Trading

Used in two senses in our report:
(1) with its normal accounting meaning, in such phrases as 'trading profit';
(2) to define those activities which are the primary responsibility of BAA's Director of Commercial Development—see paragraph 5.37.

In most cases the context will make clear the sense in which the word is used. See also Commercial.

CHAPTER 1

Summary

1.1. On 11 March 1985 the Secretary of State for Trade and Industry referred to the Commission questions regarding the efficiency, costs and standard of service of the commercial activities of the British Airports Authority. On 9 May the terms of reference were varied to confirm that the commercial activities in question were the making of arrangements by the Authority for persons other than the Authority to provide goods and services to the public, and to airlines; together with the granting of leases by the Authority. The full terms of reference are given in Chapter 2.

1.2. During the course of our inquiry the Government published a White Paper on ' Airports Policy ' (Cmnd 9542). This paper proposes sweeping changes in the ownership and regulation of airports, but our report is necessarily almost entirely concerned with the Authority's current position.

British Airports Authority

1.3. The British Airports Authority (BAA) was established by the Airports Authority Act 1965 as the owner and operator of four airports then under State control: Heathrow, Gatwick, Stansted and Prestwick, all designated Gateway International Airports. The Authority subsequently took over the regional airports at Edinburgh, Aberdeen and Glasgow; most other regional airports in the United Kingdom are owned and operated by local authorities, except eight small airports in Scotland which are operated by the Civil Aviation Authority.[1]

1.4. BAA's seven airports now handle over half of all the air transport movements in the United Kingdom and three-quarters of all air passengers. Seventy per cent of BAA's air transport movements, nearly 90 per cent of its passengers and almost all its international passengers are handled at Heathrow and Gatwick, with Heathrow taking the lion's share.

1.5. The Chairman of the Authority is appointed by the Secretary of State who, after consultation with the Chairman, also appoints the other members. Currently the Chairman, Managing Director and the Heathrow Airport Director are full-time members, and there are six non-executive part-time members. Implementation of Board policy is delegated to the Managing Director, who chairs the Executive responsible for management of the Authority's airports within the framework of approved policies.

1.6. BAA is statutorily required to provide at its airports such services and facilities as it considers necessary for their operation, except that it may not provide navigation services without Government consent. It is not specifically required to engage in commercial activities as defined in our terms of reference, but has to conduct its business so that its revenues are sufficient to cover its

---

[1] The CAA is also responsible for air traffic control, air safety, licensing of flight crew, registration of aircraft, the certification of operators and of the airworthiness of aircraft etc.

operating costs. These revenues arise from two main sources: from traffic charges to aircraft for use of BAA airports, the safe and expeditious operation of which remains the Authority's 'primary objective'; and from its commercial activities at those airports.

1.7. The Government has reserve powers to prescribe traffic charges and has agreed with the United States Government that in computing revenues that contribute to the rate of return on BAA's assets no distinction will be made between the Authority's sources of revenue including duty-free sales and other commercial activities (see paragraph 3.11). BAA has sought to develop these commercial activities both as a service to passengers and to supplement its traffic revenue. They may be broadly divided into the leasing of property, the sale of goods and services to the public and the provision of services to airlines. The Authority's policy has been to make arrangements with third parties who pay concession or licence fees for the right to supply specified goods and services at particular airports or terminals. BAA believes that this policy introduces competition and private sector expertise and enables the Authority itself to concentrate on services essential to the running of its airports. The making of these arrangements, together with the leasing by BAA of land or buildings on its airports, constitute the 'commercial activities' that are the subject of our inquiry.

Commercial activities

1.8. The first Commercial Development Director was appointed in January 1983. He is a member of the Executive with responsibility for identifying and developing commercial opportunities in all non-traffic fields. In February 1984 the Trading Department was established. The Director now has reporting to him Trading Managers, the Air Cargo Manager and the General Manager Property.[1] He thus heads a separate specialist organisation responsible broadly for appointing the concessionaires etc, managing the contractual relationships with them and for the overall success of the trading operation. He also gives advice in a 'staff' capacity to the Airport Directors who retain line responsibility for the profitability of their airports.

1.9. Two-thirds of BAA's commercial revenue in 1984-85 came from the percentage of sales paid by concessionaires who provide goods and services to the public. The concessions include duty-free and tax-free shops; bookshops and gift shops, which it is BAA policy to operate under the Authority's brand name of 'Skyshop'; some specialised retailers and a range of catering facilities. In all these cases BAA provides the premises and fixtures, but not loose or specialised fittings.

1.10. Concessions are let by competitive tender, usually for five years at a time. This allows for regular testing of the market, BAA considering that, because of space limitations in terminal buildings, it is impracticable to accommodate competing concessionaires. Direct competition in catering is particularly difficult to arrange as there is usually only one set of kitchen etc facilities per terminal. As a substitute for competition the Authority specifies in all its concession agreements the goods that are to be offered, and it exercises control over some of the prices. Concessions for supply of services to the public are treated similarly;

[1]See Appendix 3.3.

these cover up to four car rental services at an airport or terminal, car parking facilities, banking etc.

1.11. While these concessions usually involve BAA granting the right to use land or buildings they are not leases in the ordinary sense. The Authority does let land or property on ground leases or at rack rents, but even where normal landlord and tenant relationships exist the user and sub-letting provisions tend to be restrictive, to enable BAA to retain control over the operation of its airports.

1.12. Services provided to airlines, known collectively as ground handling services, include passenger, baggage and cargo handling, flight catering and aircraft towing. Most of these services are supplied by a few airlines authorised to do so by BAA, which wishes to avoid unnecessary duplication of space and handling facilities; although at Heathrow an unusually large number of airlines retain handling rights originally granted many years ago. Airlines not authorised by BAA to self-handle must therefore employ an authorised airline, or, where available, an authorised handling agent. The Authority is not directly involved in arrangements between the parties, but in most cases derives income from leasing or licensing the accommodation used for ground handling services.

1.13. Overall, rents and the provision of services to airlines produced an income to BAA of £60 million in 1984–85, which together with the concession income made a total revenue from the Authority's commercial activities of £179 million. Expenditure under this heading of £83 million thus left a profit of £96 million. By contrast, traffic services produced an income of £183 million, with an expenditure of £204 million leaving a loss of £22 million; resulting in a net profit for the Authority of nearly £75 million (see Table 4.1).

Importance of BAA's commercial activity

1.14. We comment in paragraphs 1.31 and 1.32 on the allocation of costs between commercial and traffic activities but, even allowing for any misallocation between the two headings, it is clear that without the contribution from commercial activities the Authority would be in deficit or obliged to enforce much higher traffic charges. It would also be unlikely to have been able to finance its capital expenditure almost entirely from its own resources.

1.15. BAA has said that it is committed to a policy of maximum development of its income from commercial activities consistent with the credibility of its pricing structure and its obligations as a public enterprise. Shop sizes will be increased where possible, as will the proportion of shop space allocated to tax-free sales; catering services will be improved and rental returns optimised.

1.16. Measurement of the Authority's performance in the realisation of its policy is not easy. The tables in Chapter 4 show the fluctuations in commercial income and profit per passenger adjusted for inflation and for the increase in passenger numbers. Further disaggregations are shown in an attempt to eliminate other identified causes of distortion, but there remain many extrinsic or intrinsic mechanisms which may affect the results, although neither the precise cause nor the order of its effect has been identified. The figures show an average growth in concession income per passenger over the last ten years of about 2 per cent per annum in real terms; and the Authority is budgeting for this increase to

3

continue at a similar rate. BAA's own study of its property management concluded that in general it had done as well or better than comparable indices. Comparisons with other United Kingdom and various continental airports suffer from reservations about validity, but in general they suggest that BAA airports are doing well in their commercial activities.

1.17. The available statistics provide no sure guide to the Authority's performance, and we recommend that efforts be continued to develop more meaningful and specific indicators of performance.

The role of the BAA Board

1.18. The Board's objectives are set out in the Authority's Corporate Plan, and were formally agreed with Government in 1982 (see paragraph 5.9.). The non-executive members of the BAA Board are not given specific functional responsibilities. This follows the recommendations of an internal study carried out in early 1982 with the assistance of an outside consultant, but is counter to the recommendations of a general study of nationalised industries carried out by the Central Policy Review Staff in 1981. The Board takes the view that, in general, management should respond formally through the Executive to the Board, although individual non-executive Board members are encouraged to take an informal interest in matters related to their particular expertise. There is currently no Board member with experience of retailing. Given the scale of BAA's commercial activities we think that this is unfortunate. An increase in the size of the Board—which the Chairman told us he would welcome—would help to remedy this omission. We recommend such a change.

1.19. The Board does not issue detailed guidance on reconciling operational and commercial requirements, preferring that the resolution of conflict should normally be a responsibility of airport management. The Board, however, intervenes on an *ad hoc* basis in specific difficult issues, and would normally see and approve plans for new or extended terminals. The Board should tell the Executive what range of options should be considered in planning new or redeveloped terminals, and ensure that the full range of commercial possibilities, consistent with site constraints, has been explored.

Planning guidelines

1.20. The Board issues Planning Guidelines as a starting point for determining the space needs in terminal buildings for operational and commercial purposes; these Guidelines were last revised and extended in May 1978, but are at present undergoing further revision. We think Planning Guidelines should be appropriate to the scale of the facilities likely to be planned and should be updated more frequently.

Targets

1.21. As part of the corporate planning process targets are agreed for individual managers, including the Director of Commercial Development and his subordinates. In setting challenging but feasible targets for the Authority's managers, the Board would be helped by greater understanding of the various factors which affect commercial performance.

4

Organisation

1.22. While it is too early to judge the results, we believe that the Board's 1982 decision to centralise the direction of commercial activities was soundly based. The attention so far devoted to trading should in due course be extended to other commercial activities as defined in our terms of reference, such as car parking, air cargo and property.

1.23. The primary responsibility for the performance of commercial activities remains with airport management, who have financial responsibility for all the activities at their airports. The Trading Department has sought responsibility for some capital expenditure on commercial activities but this issue remains unresolved. In our view final responsibility for all commercial activities at each airport should remain with the management of that airport.

Information and computing

1.24. Prior to 1983, when a consultancy report on its overall information processing strategy was commissioned, the Authority had encouraged a widespread interest in computers. Following the report it was accepted that there had been inadequate co-ordination and that there must be easier access to data. BAA has noted deficiencies in the management information relevant to its commercial activities and has in hand new systems to remedy the deficiencies.

1.25. BAA's first computerised property management system was installed at Heathrow in 1976 and a new system became operational at all three South-East airports during 1984. At an early stage in our inquiry BAA expressed serious concern over the new system and told us that a review was being carried out. From a paper prepared at our request it is apparent that mistakes have been made; major decisions still remain to be taken, the most important concerning Heathrow.

1.26. A separate consultants' report commissioned by the Trading Department after its establishment concluded that there were major benefits to be obtained from monitoring commercial performance and producing accurate, consistent data more quickly. It was decided to implement the proposed Trading Information System. Given our proposal that final responsibility for all commercial activities should remain with airport managers, it will be necessary to ensure that the specific trading information needs of those managers are met by this new system.

Relations with Government

1.27. BAA's principal statutory financial duties are to break even on its revenue account and to apply revenue surpluses and incur substantial capital outlays only on lines approved by the Secretary of State, to whom it reports its performance each year. There are statutory limits on borrowing. Management of its funds is highly centralised and its total outstanding debt is currently just under half the statutory limit, while it has operated well within its EFL in recent years.

1.28. In support of its primary objective of operating its airports efficiently and safely the Authority's main financial policies are to meet the targets which it

5

agrees with Government and maintain a commercial and competitive approach to its operations. The targets for return on assets, costs per passenger and productivity for 1980–81 to 1982–83 were not achieved because, the Authority told us, the expected traffic growth did not materialise. The targets for 1983–84 to 1985–86 have been revised to combine a basic underpinning element with a variable growth-related factor. The Authority expects to exceed these targets.

Budgets

1.29. For budgetary control purposes the seven airports constitute discrete business units and each prepares its own business plan. Year 1 of the final Corporate Plan is broken down into cost centres and is an instrument of financial control, but years 2 to 5 are primarily global forecasts broken down only to airports and Head Office director functions.

1.30. BAA prepares its budgets for the purposes of financial control and business planning, not as targets. The targets set within the organisation, which are expected to be consistent with the achievement of the targets agreed with Government, are more stretching than the budgets. Appendix 7.1 shows that in recent years BAA has exceeded its concession income budgets and kept within its overall expenditure budgets. This suggests to us that the Authority should review budget setting procedures to see if its budgets could be made more rigorous and challenging.

Presentation of results

1.31. A statement of income and expenditure by airport is included in the Authority's Annual Report and Accounts, split between traffic and commercial activities. This split was introduced and is maintained by Government, despite a request by BAA for the requirement to be dropped. A substantial proportion of the Authority's expenditure is not directly attributable to particular activities, and this may affect the reported results. For example, of the estimate of expenditure incurred in connection with commercial activities in 1984–85, about 33 per cent was identifiable as direct expenditure, 43 per cent as indirect and 24 per cent as common overheads. Although the present management accounting system is being replaced by the new 'general ledger' system, which will capture more data at a lower level, the problem will remain. Expenditure on items such as terminal concourses, roads and airport administration is normally allocated to traffic operations. This expenditure was undertaken in pursuance of the Authority's primary objective, and for this reason we accept the allocation as correct.

1.32. We believe that the distinction between traffic and commercial operations should continue to be drawn in BAA's accounts and that these should show separately the contributions made by particular activities at each airport to non-specific expenses and profits, and to the current cost trading profits (or losses) after a 'best judgment' allocation of non-specific expenditure, accompanied by an explanation of the basis used in making this allocation. We also believe that if privatisation takes place the airports' accounts should continue to show any subsidisation of traffic operations by commercial activities and of one airport by another.

6

Internal audit

1.33. The Board Audit Committee comprises the Managing Director and four non-executive directors, one of whom is its chairman. The Finance Director and the Chief Internal Auditor attend meetings of the Committee, which reports its findings annually to the Board. The Chief Internal Auditor, who reports to the Planning Director, is responsible for financial and efficiency audits including the audit of concessions, in accordance with an annual programme approved by the Managing Director. We consider he should report directly to a Board member. Audit reports appear well prepared, although the time taken to respond to them is lengthening. We should like to see the Audit Committee more closely involved in overseeing internal audit, the effectiveness of which depends on continued support by the Managing Director and senior management.

1.34. The Chief Internal Auditor is graded below the airport general managers. While we have no reason to believe that this grading is inappropriate, we hope that the Authority will keep the grading of all internal audit posts under careful review.

Investment appraisal

1.35. Investment in commercial activities has averaged £21 million per annum (1983–84 prices) over the last eight years. Projects over £15 million at Heathrow and Gatwick, and over £5 million elsewhere, must be submitted to the Department of Transport for approval; some such developments have included a commercial element. Projects over £5 million require approval by the BAA Board; below that level authority is delegated to the Managing Director and by him (for projects up to £1 million) to Airport Directors.

1.36. All projects above £30,000 are subject to financial appraisal, which is carried out in accordance with Government guidelines and requirements, which specify an overall return of 5 per cent on all new investment. For service projects from which no direct profits are sought (eg to meet traffic, safety or security needs) the normal financial appraisal cannot be carried out, but appraisals are required of alternative methods of achieving a particular service standard, or an evaluation of the cost and financial impact of the project, with preliminary cost benefit analysis where appropriate.

1.37. The application of the guidelines is monitored by the submission to Head Office of the appraisals for all projects approved by Directors under their delegated powers. The Finance Economics Branch at Head Office has also recently embarked on a systematic system of back-checks on investment decisions. In a mixed commercial/operational development the commercial element is not separately appraised. BAA has argued that options for provision of commercial facilities have been constrained by the nature of the sites available, but we think this argument can be overstated and recommend that all options should be formally appraised.

1.38. Appraisals of a sample of investments in specific commercial facilities and in combined projects show that the majority had been the subject of formal investment appraisal, but only a few contained sensitivity analyses. The recent adoption of revised guidelines for project assessment should lead to some improvement in technique, particularly in relation to smaller projects.

Concessions

1.39. Concessions are let by tender, usually for a period of five years, and sometimes with an option for the Authority to extend by three years. Concessionaires normally pay the Authority a percentage of total turnover, or different percentages of turnover for specific product groups. This is sometimes supported (notably for car hire) by a guarantee of a minimum payment irrespective of turnover. For duty-free and tax-free concessions there are provisions which enable the agreed percentages to be varied. There are also provisions which allow BAA to exercise control over concessionaires' operations by specifying retail prices, ranges to be stocked and opening hours.

1.40. The major rights to sell goods and services to the public on BAA airports are held by relatively few companies: the dominant concessionaires are Allders International and Trusthouse Forte (THF) for duty-free and tax-free shops, THF for catering and duty-paid shops, Avis, Hertz and Godfrey Davis Europcar for car hire and NCP for car parks. The same firms are also prominent concessionaires at the six largest local authority airports.

1.41. Concessionaires criticised the short period of a concession and the lack of participation by the concessionaire in capital investment. Allders and THF considered a longer period would encourage staff and make for better management: Allders stressed the problems caused by stocking an airport duty-free shop (on a five-year concession) from an off-airport warehouse (typically on a 21-year lease). THF thought that participation by concessionaires in capital investment would result in facilities better matched to market requirements; the concessionaire would be more responsive to changes in demand and stimulated to better performance.

1.42. BAA thinks that a five-year concession is a suitable balance between the need for regular tendering (to maintain competition) and the stability required by a concessionaire to develop its business. It is also an appropriate period because of the rapidly changing nature of the market. Given this, BAA considers that investment by concessionaires would lead to difficulties when concessions changed hands. It recognises that time-limited concessions cause problems for management and staff and it encourages new concessionaires to take over the staff of the previous concessionaire. In the case of catering concessions the Authority is relaxing its control of prices and intends to introduce an incentive scheme which, if successful, may be extended to other areas.

1.43. We recognise that five-year contracts may not be in the best interest of concessionaires but given the monopoly rights in effect granted by BAA we believe all contracts should remain subject to regular tendering. The question of capital investment being undertaken by catering concessionaires should be kept under review.

1.44. The Authority also receives some income from services provided to airlines by third parties (see paragraph 1.12 and Table 9.5). This income is derived from a variety of arrangements and includes rentals of facilities and licence fees (some fixed sums and others based on a percentage of turnover). Licences are generally granted for three years subject to six months' notice of termination. The licensee is restricted to specified services, for which he must obtain contracts. The Authority will grant new licences only upon representation by the airlines. Licences are not subject to tendering, but are granted to those nominated by the airlines.

Rents and property

1.45. Property accounts for about two-thirds of BAA's assets invested in commercial facilities, the rents from which produce about £25 million a year, with a similar amount charged to tenants for services. Nearly three-quarters of the rent and services income is generated at Heathrow. Property grants, as distinct from concessions, may take the form of licences (such as those for check-in desks), short-term tenancies, long leases or ground leases. In most cases payment is a fixed annual sum and not as with concessions a percentage of the occupier's turnover.

1.46. BAA interprets its statutory duty to provide facilities for the operation of its airports as preventing it from investing in activities not related to an airport and from letting property in central areas for such activities. BAA retains various parcels of land for which no precise airport-related development has been identified and it considers acquisition of sites adjacent to airports for possible future developments. We received complaints from tenants that restrictive conditions in BAA leases and tenancies discourage the best use of land and buildings, and that when an existing tenant seeks release from a restrictive term so as to benefit financially the Authority will only consider approval subject to receiving some payment itself.

1.47. As a result of the recent recession there is some unlet office accommodation at Heathrow and Gatwick. At Heathrow this unlet accommodation, currently with a potential rent of some half a million pounds a year, is forecast to increase temporarily following the opening of Terminal 4. Allowing however for the dislocation attendant upon the redevelopment at that airport the amount of vacant accommodation is considered by BAA not to be far out of line with that accompanying a normal turnover in tenancies. Its projections suggest that the present excess supply of office accommodation at the two airports should be absorbed within a few years. There is also some under-utilisation of cargo facilities constructed on land leased from BAA at Heathrow.

1.48. BAA charges open market rents or, for new accommodation, the economic rent where that is higher; and hybrid rents, with an element linked to turnover, in cases such as hotels and fuel leases. Market rents are determined with reference to the off-airport market and to on-airport demand. In general rents at Heathrow have increased over the last ten years more rapidly than elsewhere. Office rents in the central terminal area at Heathrow are above those in surrounding towns; BAA says that this is attributable to economic market forces. British Airways, however, argued that rent and licence fees are forced up by

9

under-provision of the facilities needed by airlines. We consider BAA's policies for determining rental levels to be reasonable. Charges for licences are based on the costs incurred in providing and maintaining the facility plus the cost of the space used.

Aircraft fuel supply

1.49. In 1984 the Authority made new arrangements, including a 21-year lease, for the supply of aviation fuel through the common pipe network at Heathrow. The old arrangements were due to expire in 1991, but the need to arrange for the supply of fuel to Terminal 4 provided an opportunity to re-negotiate them. Fuel suppliers' airport turnover is about £450 million per annum and in addition to their rents some suppliers were also paying BAA a gallonage fee. The new arrangements provide for a rent indexed to RPI, with further increases related to passenger growth, and overall represent a [*   ] increase in revenue to BAA. The Authority insisted on clauses in the agreement permitting suitable new entrants to join the consortium, but the effectiveness of this agreement can only be judged when British Airways' current application to join is determined.

1.50. At Gatwick BAA would like a similar new arrangement with the eight oil companies who form a consortium and pay the Authority rent and a gallonage charge. British Caledonian told us that the lack of one common pipe network at Gatwick increased costs and that the method widely adopted in the United States of one agent operating a common system was more economic and permitted competition between fuel suppliers. We consider that BAA should increase competition in the supply of fuel at Gatwick when the present fuel arrangements are renegotiated.

Competition in sales to the public

1.51. The extent of competition at point of sale is limited by lack of space in airport terminals. BAA seeks to promote competition both by granting concessions for relatively short periods and by widening the range of goods offered rather than by accommodating directly competing concessionaires.

1.52. However, even where competition would be possible, either directly or through promotional activities, BAA effectively restricts or prevents it. BAA considers it is obliged to protect against off-airport competition the concessionaires who have paid for the right to operate on the airport and whose activities there are regulated, although in most cases there is no term in the contract granting an exclusive right.

1.53. BAA has in the past offered the duty- and tax-free outlets in a terminal as two separate concessions, but it is now the Authority's practice to offer them as a single concession. Customs and Excise have resisted separate operators for such outlets within one terminal because of staff shortages. However, they told us that they would consider competing operators if it was shown to be in the public interest and if adequate facilities could be provided. Airlines complained to us that BAA prevents them promoting their in-flight duty-free prices at their check-in desks.

---

* Figure omitted. See note on page iv.

1.54. It is BAA practice to let all catering concessions in one terminal together, primarily because existing terminals have only one set of back-up facilities. An exception to this constraint will be Terminal 4 at Heathrow, where the design makes it possible to have competing operators both for catering and for duty- and tax-free sales.

1.55. Because of the protected market in which airport concessionaires operate BAA feels it necessary to exercise varying degrees of control over their prices. In the case of duty-free goods BAA, having specified the range to be carried, requires a minimum saving to the customer of 37·5 per cent on spirits and tobacco products against the average High Street price as determined by the Authority. Prices are uniform at all BAA airports. We received no complaints from concessionaires about the exercise of this power. For tax-free goods BAA requires that prices should not exceed local retail prices less VAT. Until recently the Authority controlled the price and specification of everything sold by catering concessionaires but, in the interests of simplicity and flexibility, it now controls only 'core' items leaving the concessionaire to add other products subject to BAA approval.

1.56. The duty-paid Skyshops are required to stock BAA's 'own brand' merchandise and a specified range of brand leaders (see paragraph 4.3). There is no specification of the range of magazines to be stocked; we received a complaint about the paucity of choice. Skyshops and specialist shops may not exceed the manufacturers' recommended or suggested retail price or, failing that, the High Street price. Although concessionaires were said by BAA usually to be content with the Skyshop title, we think it would be better for both staff and customers if shops traded under their own names.

1.57. At all its airports except Glasgow BAA sets the prices for car parking. In an attempt to ration demand there are relatively high charges for the central area at Heathrow, whilst there are very low charges at Stansted to encourage use of the airport. At Glasgow NCP sets the prices subject to the Authority's approval under a 99-year contract that BAA inherited when it took over the airport.

1.58. The agreements for car rental require prices not to exceed the concessionaires' 'national rate', or the central London rate in the case of Heathrow. The concessionaires interpret national rate to mean the one-way rate, although reductions are offered by their off-airport offices when the car is returned to that office. A high proportion of airport rentals are in fact returned to the airport of hire. The Authority told us that it would review the terms of its car hire contracts in respect of the national rates. We think that customers should be charged on the basis appropriate to the type of hire involved.

1.59. One off-airport operator complained of inadequate signposting to the rental pick-up point, a prohibition on advertising its services on BAA airports and on having 'meet and greet' staff for pre-booked arriving customers, or car key deposit boxes for departing passengers. It had offered to pay BAA a percentage of any extra business that resulted from the presence of its representatives on the airport, but the offer had been refused. The Authority told us it would improve the signposting. The prohibition of advertising by off-airport firms competing with concessionaires is we consider unjustified: the limited

11

advertising space should be available without discrimination to all advertisements which are 'honest, decent, legal and truthful'.

1.60. Each banking concessionaire is granted exclusivity within its terminal, except at Gatwick where two banks operate. The Authority requires the concessionaires at the South-East airports to encash cheques drawn on other clearing banks without charge and intends to extend this requirement to the Scottish airports.

1.61. BAA told us that it was concerned at the limited number of concessionaires whom it found suitable to tender at its airports, particularly for catering and duty-free shops. It had a predisposition in favour of companies which had shown themselves able to operate successfully under exacting airport conditions. There has been public comment that at every BAA airport the parking facilities are operated by NCP, apart from Stansted where the Authority operates its own car parks. We believe the concentration amongst concessionaires is a product of the tendering process. The Authority should make every effort to attract a greater number of tenders, in particular by ensuring that the time allowed for preparation of tenders is adequate for a new tenderer and that full information is provided at the outset.

Competition in services to airlines

1.62. Originally any airline at Heathrow could provide its own ground handling services (see paragraphs 4.6 to 4.8 and 11.46 *et seq*). In 1969 BAA's attempts to introduce an independent handling agent failed in the face of industrial action. As problems arose from the airside proliferation of vehicles and equipment a freeze was placed in 1978 on further self-handling, which left eight airlines with full self-handling rights. These airlines may also sell their services to other airlines, but only at the terminal at which they themselves operate; exceptionally British Airways may provide services at all terminals. The right of airlines to provide certain specific ground services has since 1978 been controlled by licence and in addition some third party suppliers are licensed to give specialised cleaning, aircraft catering etc services.

1.63. In 1982 BAA invited tenders from the eight airlines with 'grandfather' rights to become the 'nominated handler'—the handler of last resort who would be obliged to provide services on demand to any airline at any terminal. In return BAA was to ensure that the range of services offered by the existing self-handlers was not increased nor was any other airline to provide such services. Aer Lingus became the nominated handler in 1982; the formal contract runs for five years from January 1984, and stipulates payment to BAA of a percentage on any new business. We were told that Aer Lingus had obtained no new business during the currency of the contract.

1.64. British Midland Airways (BMA) complained to us that it was not allowed to self-handle, although in terms of aircraft movements it was the second largest carrier at Heathrow. It was faced with choosing between British Airways, with which it is in direct competition, or a foreign airline, Aer Lingus. It had no complaint about the Aer Lingus service, but believed it could do its own handling at little over half the price, to the benefit of its competitive position. We consider

12

that, on the expiry of the Aer Lingus licence as nominated handler, the opportunity to tender should be open to any airline using Heathrow and to any outside handling agency.

1.65. BMA does not accept the Authority's argument that to allow one new self-handler would encourage a flood of applications, nor that there need be any net addition to the equipment needed airside. The Authority told us that it would review its handling policy at Heathrow one year after Terminal 4 opens. We consider that BAA should survey the use of airside equipment at Heathrow and allow airlines with handling rights there to offer their services at any terminal where this would improve utilisation.

1.66. BAA has limited the number of handling agents at Gatwick to three, British Airways, British Caledonian and Gatwick Handling (GH). The latter was a joint venture shared between Dan-Air and Laker Airways; when Laker collapsed Britannia Airways wanted to buy into GH, but Dan-Air would not accept it as an equal partner and Laker's share was bought by two American airlines. BAA has a reserve right to approve the prices GH charges. Britannia feels disadvantaged in having to pay what it regards as higher charges than a handling agent would ask in order to buy services from its competitors. BAA told us that it would review the situation at Gatwick after the new North Terminal opened.

1.67. We believe that the degree of choice available to airlines without self-handling rights at Heathrow and Gatwick is inadequate. We recommend that the Authority should arrange matters at both airports so that in each terminal an airline without self-handling rights has a choice of at least two handlers, neither of which is an airline with which it is in direct competition. In making these arrangements BAA should not limit itself to airlines with existing self-handling rights, and should take account of the charges made to airlines and the cost savings achievable.

1.68. In-flight catering at Heathrow can be provided by any of the self-handlers, plus El-Al, four licensed off-airport caterers and Trusthouse Forte. The off-airport caterers pay a percentage to BAA although the handling airlines and El-Al do not, and their licences are restricted to specific services. New licences are not issued except at the request of the Airline Operators Committees at Heathrow and Gatwick, or at the request of airlines at other airports.

Basis of tendering

1.69. The basis upon which concessionaires' bids have to be made is designed to maximise BAA income rather than to minimise charges to the consumer. This is consistent with the Authority's policy to maximise revenue but may not be consistent with its obligations as a public enterprise (see paragraph 11.79). An alternative approach might be to let concession contracts on a different basis, such as a fixed rental and prescribed standards of service with the tenders being judged on the lowest prices proposed to be charged to customers.

Air traffic services

1.70. Air traffic services at BAA airports are at present provided by the CAA (see paragraph 1.6). It might be difficult to introduce a contractor other than th CAA into the London area, but we recommend that the Authority should consider the possibility of doing so at its smaller airports, in order to reduce the costs of these services to airlines.

Manpower efficiency

1.71. Most staff engaged on commercial activities are employed by concessionaires, but these are outside our terms of reference. BAA employs 292 staff on commercial activities; 116 of them are also partly engaged on activities beyond our inquiry. It was therefore impracticable to establish meaningful productivity measures for BAA staff for commercial activities alone. Two of the performance targets agreed with Government apply to BAA staff generally and call for a reduction in real terms of costs per terminal passenger and an increase in terminal passengers per payroll hour. Both targets were exceeded in 1983–84.

1.72. The Corporate Plan includes a manpower plan with projections for five years. These show an increase in total staff numbers of 6·8 per cent—against a forecast traffic growth of 18 per cent—mainly to reflect developments at Heathrow Terminal 4 and at Gatwick North Terminal. We saw no evidence of over- or under-staffing and we are satisfied that the overall downward pressure on staffing numbers stemming from the performance targets has been effective.

1.73. Vacancies are normally notified internally and, where the necessary expertise may not be available among existing staff, are advertised externally. Ten members of staff currently employed in the Trading Department were recruited from external sources. All jobs below senior management are subject to job evaluation schemes. A productivity scheme based on the ratio of added value to employee costs has produced payments to individuals over the last three years of about 10 per cent of basic pay.

1.74. The Authority has devoted considerable resources to training its staff during the past three years. We hope that the Authority will be able to carry out an objective assessment of the effects of this training on its commercial activities.

1.75. The Authority has a statutory duty to consult with appropriate trade unions. The machinery of negotiation and consultation operates throughout the organisation (see Appendix 12.3) and the secretaries of the trade union sides of the committees for Heathrow, Gatwick and the Scottish airports are engaged full time on trade union duties. There has been no industrial dispute involving BAA staff engaged on commercial activities and during our inquiry we have been aware of a feeling of common purpose among staff at all levels.

Quality of service

1.76. We are required to investigate and report, *inter alia,* whether in carrying on its commercial activities the Authority could improve the service provided. Whether commercial service and commercial profit are complementary or whether they have to be 'traded off' against each other is important to our

14

consideration of the quality of BAA's service. The Authority argues that increased sales and profitability are an accurate medium- and long-term reflection of customer satisfaction. We accept that where increased revenue does not result from higher prices in real terms, but from an increase in the goods and services bought per passenger, it is an indicator of customer satisfaction. BAA should, however, continue to look separately at the individual performance of specific activities.

1.77. The Authority uses several means to control and monitor quality of service. Standards may be laid down for general guidance (eg the passenger service standards, expressed in terms of waiting times and areas per passenger) or incorporated into concession contracts or the various forms of property grant; the observance of these can be directly monitored. In other cases the quality of service provided is assessed by various survey techniques, and by statistical analysis to produce performance indicators. Targets are set for improvements: these may take such forms as a reduction in waiting times or in complaint levels.

1.78. Provision should continue to be made for the representation of passengers' interests by Passenger Services sub-Committees. Given the variety of roles which the Airport Consultative Committees are required to play, consideration should be given to increasing the independence of the Passenger Services sub-Committees by separating their funding and the appointment of their members from those of the Consultative Committees. The results of passenger opinion surveys should also be made available to them.

Overall assessment

1.79. BAA is faced to an unusual degree with the need constantly to decide between competing claims for its limited space and facilities. It is required by statute to 'have regard to the development of air transport and to efficiency, economy and safety of operation'. The Authority's first priority is therefore the safe and expeditious handling of aircraft at its airports, together with the passengers and cargo they carry. As these have increased—and are forecast to increase still further—so the demands for space on the airports to handle this traffic have increased. Scope for enlarging many of the Authority's airports is however limited by a variety of factors, notably physical and environmental.

1.80. Although BAA is not specifically required to engage in the commercial activities which are the subject of our inquiry it is nevertheless faced with another call on its space, the growing expectation among air travellers that they will find at major airports catering, shopping etc facilities extending beyond the obvious essential services. BAA told us that where considerations of space are concerned traffic interests must take priority. However BAA will always face pressure to increase the scope of its commercial activities because these raise substantial revenue. This revenue finances investment in new or improved facilities—traffic and commercial—and it subsidises the charges BAA levies on aircraft.

1.81. There is thus a constant need to reconcile competing demands and it is in the undeniable attractions to the Authority of the commercial revenue to be earned that a danger lies; this revenue is earned at airports which are in practice virtually closed markets and thus potentially liable to monopolistic exploitation.

15

1.82. We have had to bear all this in mind when considering the Authority's commercial performance. We have concluded that we could not safely reach a decision based only on the figures available to us; too many so far unquantified factors affected their movement over recent years. However, from our visits to airports, from the evidence we received and in the light of the limited criticisms we have to make as a result of our extensive enquiries into the Authority's commercial activities, it is our judgment that these are conducted in a generally satisfactory manner.

1.83. Accordingly we conclude that while there are areas in which the Authority could and should improve upon its present practices, and while the potential danger inherent in a near monopoly trading position can only be heightened by the current drive to enlarge and improve commercial activities, these activities are not conducted in a way that operates against the public interest. However Professor George, a member of the group which dealt with this inquiry, while agreeing with our other conclusions dissented from this finding. He believes that the way in which BAA has effectively restricted or prevented competition to its concessionaires does operate against the public interest, and that a partial remedy for this is to be found in the recommendations we have made.

1.84. Our detailed conclusions and recommendations are summarised in Chapter 14 and here we only draw attention to the fact that we have necessarily dealt with the present position at BAA airports, not the situation that is proposed in the White Paper 'Airports Policy'. We have no reason to believe, however, that our conclusions would not be equally relevant in the new situation, when additional pressures may make it even more difficult for the Authority's successor to hold a proper balance between an entrepreneurial approach to commercial activities and a possible abuse of a monopoly position.

CHAPTER 2

Introduction

2.1. On 11 March 1985 the Department of Trade and Industry sent to the Commission the following reference:

The Secretary of State, in exercise of his powers under section 11(1)(*a*) and (*b*) of the Competition Act 1980, hereby refers to the Monopolies and Mergers Commission ('the Commission') the questions set out below relating to the efficiency and costs of and the service provided by the British Airports Authority ('the Authority') in its commercial activities.

For the purpose of this reference:

'commercial activities' means the following activities carried on by the Authority, namely:

(*a*) the making of arrangements, whether by concession or otherwise, to sell goods by retail, provide public catering facilities, operate chauffeur driven car hire services, operate public car parks and provide other services to the public;

(*b*) the making of arrangements, whether by licence, contract or otherwise, for the provision of services to airlines including the provision of services by one airline to another;

(*c*) the granting of leases of land including the granting of consents to assignments of such leases and the general administration of such leases.

The Commission shall upon this reference investigate and report on the following questions:

(1) whether in carrying on its commercial activities the Authority could improve its efficiency or reduce its costs or improve the service provided, with particular reference to:

(*a*) the scope for increasing competition at the point of sale, having regard to security and safety requirements and the need to ensure the comfort and convenience of passengers and the efficient operation of the airport;

(*b*) the methods and practices of the Authority in selecting the persons to whom concessions are to be granted including the Authority's procedures for inviting and accepting tenders, the imposition on concessionaires by the Authority of contractual terms relating to the price, nature, range and quality of the goods and services to be provided by concessionaires and the award and renewal by the Authority of contracts;

(*c*) the monitoring and control by the Authority of the standard of services provided to passengers by concessionaires;

(d) the administration and management by the Authority of leases of land where the Authority is the lessor; and

(2) whether in relation to any matter falling within the question set out in (1) above, other than the matter of the application of the Authority's revenues to finance any of the Authority's activities which are not commercial activities, the Authority is pursuing a course of conduct which operates against the public interest.

The Commission shall report upon this reference within a period of six months beginning on the date hereof.

11 March 1985

(signed) **M J Vile**
An Assistant Secretary
Department of Trade and Industry

2.2. On 9 May 1985 the Department sent to the Commission a variation of the reference defining more precisely the subject of the inquiry, which was the making of arrangements by the Authority for the provision by third parties of services to the public and to airlines. The variation read:

Whereas by a Reference dated 11 March 1985 the Secretary of State, in exercise of his powers under section 11(1)(*a*) and (*b*) of the Competition Act 1980, referred to the Monopolies and Mergers Commission certain questions relating to the efficiency and costs of and the service provided by the British Airports Authority in its commercial activities:

Now therefore, the Secretary of State, in exercise of his powers under section 11(6) of the said Act, hereby varies the said Reference by substituting the following for paragraphs (*a*) and (*b*) of the definition of ' commercial activities ' in the said Reference:

(*a*) the making of arrangements, whether by concession or otherwise, for persons other than the Authority to sell goods by retail, provide public catering facilities, operate chauffeur driven car hire services, operate public car parks and provide other services to the public;

(*b*) the making of arrangements, whether by licence, contract or otherwise, for persons other than the Authority to provide services to airlines, including, without prejudice to the generality of the foregoing, arrangements for any airline to provide services to airlines.

9 May 1985

(signed) **M J Vile**
An Assistant Secretary
Department of Trade and Industry

2.3. The Chairman of the Commission, acting under section 11(9) of the Competition Act 1980 and Part II of Schedule 3 to the Fair Trading Act 1973, directed on 12 March 1985 that the functions of the Commission in relation to the reference should be discharged through a group of six members including himself as Chairman. The composition of the group is indicated in the list of members which prefaces this report.

2.4. Representatives of the British Airports Authority (BAA) supplied a great deal of written evidence, and attended two hearings at the Commission. Members of the Commission visited Gatwick, Heathrow and Glasgow airports; officials of the Commission made detailed enquiries at all seven BAA airports and at six major local authority airports.

2.5. The reference was advertised in the following publications:

Daily Telegraph	*The Times*
Financial Times	*Travel Trade Gazette*
Flight International	*London and Edinburgh Gazettes*

As a result both of these advertisements, and of direct invitations, evidence was received from a large number of organisations. The list in Appendix 2.1 indicates those who provided written evidence, those who attended formal hearings with the Commission, and those who provided information at meetings with staff.

2.6. We are most grateful to all those who helped us, in particular to those representatives of BAA on whom the main burden of our enquiries inevitably fell. Some of the evidence we received was of a confidential nature; our report contains only such information as we consider necessary for an understanding of our conclusions.

2.7. During the course of our inquiry the Government published a White Paper entitled 'Airports Policy'.[1] This contained proposals for the future ownership and regulation of airports. Our report deals mainly with the Authority as we have found it and not as it may evolve (but see paragraphs 14.6 and 14.7).

---

[1] Cmnd 9542, June 1985.

CHAPTER 3

The British Airports Authority

3.1. This chapter describes briefly the origin of the Authority, its statutory background, the seven airports that it owns and operates, the commercial activities that it carries out at those airports and the shape of its organisation. Some of these matters are developed more fully in subsequent chapters.

Statutory background

3.2. BAA was established in 1965 under the Airports Authority Act of that year. At that time the State owned and operated 22 civil airports and it was decided that four of these—Heathrow, Gatwick, Stansted, and Prestwick, designated Gateway International Airports—should come under the ownership of the new Authority which commenced operations on 1 April 1966. Others, identified as regional airports, were transferred to their respective local authorities; while the Civil Aviation Authority (CAA) subsequently took over, and still operates, the eight small ' Highlands and Islands ' airports in Scotland.[1]

3.3. BAA subsequently acquired Edinburgh airport in 1971, followed by Aberdeen and Glasgow both in 1975. Thus BAA now owns and operates three airports in the South-East and four under its separate Scottish Airports Division.

3.4. BAA currently operates under the terms of the Airports Authority Act 1975 (the 1975 Act). Section 2(1) of that Act provides that ' it shall be the duty of the Authority to provide at its aerodromes such services and facilities as are in its opinion necessary or desirable for their operation, but the Authority shall not provide any navigation services except with the consent in writing of the Secretary of State '. Other United Kingdom airports are free, within the standards prescribed by the CAA, to provide navigation services themselves and all airports may contract their provision to private companies, subject again to CAA standards and, in the case of BAA, the consent of the Secretary of State. Navigation services at all BAA airports, however, are currently provided by the CAA. Section 2 of the Act also requires the Authority to ' have regard to the development of air transport and to efficiency, economy and safety of operation '. BAA has in agreement with the Government established corporate objectives and performance targets (see paragraphs 5.9 and 5.12).

3.5. The Authority is further empowered, with the Secretary of State's consent, to acquire or discontinue the use of any airport. Although it acquired three regional airports under the original 1965 Act, as noted above, there have been no acquisitions or closures during the currency of the 1975 Act.

3.6. BAA is also required to provide ' adequate facilities for consultation ' with the users of its airports, with relevant local authorities and with

---

[1] The CAA is also responsible for air traffic control, air safety, licensing of flight crew, registration of aircraft, certification of operators and of the airworthiness of aircraft, advice to the Government on civil aviation matters etc (see also paragraphs 3.9 and 3.10).

20

organisations representing the interests of persons in the areas concerned. It has established a Consultative Committee and an Airline Operators Committee at each of its airports; airlines, aviation interests and travel agents are represented on a Consultation Co-ordination Council. There are also some associated groups dealing with particular interests.

3.7. BAA's financial duties are dealt with in section 3 of the 1975 Act, which requires it to conduct its business so that its revenue is not less than sufficient to meet the charges properly chargeable to revenue, taking one year with another. The Secretary of State's approval is required for the lines on which substantial outlay on capital account is incurred. The Authority has in fact financed its operations wholly from internal resources for 13 of the 19 years of its existence and up to March 1985 has paid £92 million in corporation tax.

3.8. Certain other statutes specifically apply to the Authority in the operation of its airports, such as the Civil Aviation Act 1982 which *inter alia* deals with the regulation of aircraft noise. Security measures arising from the United Kingdom's adherence to international conventions are reflected in the Aviation Security Act 1982; security personnel represent the largest single category of staff employed by the Authority.[1] BAA is required by this Act to pay for police services which are provided at each airport by the local force.

3.9. BAA cannot choose which airlines operate from its airports. The CAA licenses all United Kingdom airlines and internal routes, while international air services are operated under the provision of bilateral agreements negotiated by the Governments of the countries concerned and which specify the airports to be used. BAA does, however, have the right to deny the use of its airports to any airline which refuses to comply with the Authority's Conditions of Use.

3.10. All United Kingdom airports also have to be licensed by the CAA and the Government has reserve powers under the Air Navigation Order 1980 to prescribe the landing fees charged. An agreement between the United Kingdom and the United States of America of 23 July 1977 (known as Bermuda 2) requires that these charges shall (in brief) be just and reasonable, shall not discriminate in favour of British airlines and may reflect but shall not exceed the full cost of providing the facilities and services required.

3.11. The level of charges at Heathrow was recently the subject of litigation between the Authority and some airlines. Associated with the settlement of this litigation there was a Memorandum of Understanding dated 6 April 1983 between HM Government and the Government of the United States. Paragraph 4(*c*) of this memorandum states:

In formulating financial targets with the BAA, HMG acknowledges the need to secure efficient use of the public resources employed by the BAA, and looks for no more than a reasonable rate of return on investment. In computing revenues that contribute to the rate of return on assets, no distinction will be made as to the sources of revenue, including duty-free sales and other commercial revenues.

---

[1] At 31 March 1984 BAA employed 1,870 persons on security out of a total of 6,929 staff.

21

BAA airports

3.12. The 1978 White Paper on Airport Policy defined four categories of United Kingdom airport:

Gateway International Airports—with a wide range and frequency of international services (Category A);

Regional Airports—with scheduled international short-haul services, charter services and domestic services (Category B);

Local Airports—with local and domestic feeder services and some charter services (Category C); and

General Aviation Aerodromes—concerned primarily with the provision of general aviation facilities (Category D). [1]

The paper concluded that there was demand for only one other Gateway International Airport in addition to the four already operated by BAA and that this should be at Manchester, a local authority airport.[2]

3.13. The seven BAA airports thus comprise two disparate groups serving different markets. The London and South-East group (Heathrow, Gatwick and Stansted) serve most of the United Kingdom's international flights, as well as much domestic traffic. By far the most important of these three airports is Heathrow, which was taken over from the RAF at the end of the war and formally opened as a civil airport in May 1946. In that year 63,000 passengers used Heathrow on 2,046 air transport movements.[3] Last year Heathrow was used by over 29 million passengers—making it the sixth busiest in the world; 24 million of these were international passengers—far more than at any other airport in the world. Heathrow now handles over 270,000 ATMs a year, nearly all of which are scheduled services, at a peak time rate of more than one a minute. It also handles over half a million tonnes of cargo a year, which on a value basis (over £16·5 billion) makes it Britain's most important port. Some 46,000 people are employed at Heathrow, although less than 10 per cent of these work for the Authority.

3.14. Gatwick was a small public airport before the war, after which it was chosen as London's second airport. With 14 million passengers and 141,000 ATMs a year it is now the second busiest airport in the United Kingdom and the fourth busiest in Europe: in terms of international passengers it is the fourth busiest in the world. About 40 per cent of the ATMs and 60 per cent of the passengers are on non-scheduled flights, eg charters.

3.15. The third BAA South-East airport is at Stansted, which was not released from United States Air Force use until 1957. More than half of its current annual 12,800 ATMs and 90 per cent of its half a million passengers are on non-scheduled flights and in addition it is much used by general aviation. On 5 June

---

[1]Scheduled services are services publicly advertised by an airline through its issued timetables. Non-scheduled services are other flights by airlines carrying passengers or cargo, eg charter flights. 'General aviation' covers other civil flights, eg flying clubs, air taxis, training and pleasure flights etc.

[2]We were told that there is no current definitive list categorising all United Kingdom airports, but that Luton (owned by the local authority) is considered a Gateway International Airport.

[3]An air transport movement, or ATM, is a landing or a take-off by an aircraft operating a scheduled or non-scheduled service. The number of ATMs at an airport will therefore be less than the total of all aircraft movements at the airport (see footnote (1) to paragraph 3.12).

1985 the Government announced its intention that Stansted should be developed, initially to a capacity of seven to eight million passengers per annum (mppa) and, eventually, to 15 mppa.

3.16. BAA's Scottish airports (Prestwick, Edinburgh, Glasgow and Aberdeen) are quite different in scale and character from the London and South-East group. Prestwick, 29 miles south-west of Glasgow, is the fourth of the BAA Gateway International Airports. In the early post-war years it represented an important facility for North Atlantic flights but the longer ranges achieved by modern aircraft have reduced its importance, although it has recently been named as the site for the only Scottish ' free port '. Last year it handled 314,000 passengers on 3,100 ATMs, although the total number of flights including military flights and general aviation was over 30,000.

3.17. The other three airports in the Authority's Scottish Division are the regional airports of Edinburgh with 34,000 ATMs, Glasgow with 55,000 and Aberdeen with 82,000 (of which 46,000 were helicopter movements mainly associated with North Sea oil operations). By contrast Manchester, the largest non-BAA airport, had 70,000 ATMs last year. No non-BAA airport in the United Kingdom exceeded two million passengers in the year, except Manchester with six million.

3.18. In total BAA's seven airports handle 60 per cent of United Kingdom ATMs, 75 per cent of air passengers and 85 per cent of air cargo tonnage. A comparison of BAA airports with other major United Kingdom airports and with some foreign airports is at Appendix 3.1.

Commercial activities

3.19. BAA in its published accounts identifies two kinds of revenue: from traffic and from commercial activities. Traffic revenue is generated by the charges made by the Authority in the pursuit of its ' primary objective '[1]—to respond to the present and future needs of air transport, and to operate its airports efficiently and profitably so as to permit the safe and expeditious landing and take-off of aircraft.

3.20. The 1975 Act does not specifically require BAA to engage in commercial activities, but as noted in paragraph 3.4 the Act requires the Authority to provide ' such services and facilities as are in its opinion necessary or desirable '; and it also empowers BAA ' to do anything which is calculated to facilitate the discharge of its duties '. Under these provisions the Authority has developed commercial activities at its airports, mainly to meet the needs of passengers, and to raise revenue which supplements that obtained from landing etc fees. These commercial activities may be broadly divided into the leasing by the Authority of land or buildings to airlines and other airport-related interests, the sale of goods and services to the public and the provision of services to airlines.

3.21. The Authority's policy has been to make arrangements for third parties to sell goods or provide services in return for a consideration. This policy is believed by BAA to introduce competition and private sector expertise, while

[1]See the 1985 Corporate Plan, paragraph 5.9.

leaving the Authority to provide essential airport facilities and services: fire and rescue, security and snow clearance are, for example, considered fundamental to safe operation and are provided by BAA at all its airports.

3.22. Payments received under these arrangements with third parties and from the leasing of land or buildings constitute the Authority's revenue from commercial activities. These activities are the subject of our inquiry; they are described more fully in the following chapter.

Organisation[1]

3.23. Section 1 of the 1975 Act provides for the Secretary of State to appoint the Chairman of the Authority and to appoint a Deputy Chairman and not more than eight and not less than four other members after consultation with the Chairman. At present the Authority has three full-time Board members—the Chairman, Managing Director, and the Heathrow Airport Director; and six part-time members, one of whom is required by the Act to have special knowledge of the circumstances of Scotland. Full-time appointments are usually for five years and part-time appointments for two or three years. Board meetings are normally held monthly and at least three times a year are held at BAA airports in rotation.

3.24. There are three Committees of the Board: the Audit Committee with five members, four of whom including the chairman are non-executive, with the duty of ensuring the sufficiency of accounts and finances and the maintenance of a direct link with the external auditors; the Design Committee which considers architecture, design philosophy and criteria; and the Salary Committee of part-time members who review and make recommendations on salaries and allowances for senior management and full-time Board members.

3.25. The implementation of Board policies is delegated to the Managing Director who chairs the Executive; the members of this are the Directors for Heathrow, Gatwick and Stansted, the Scottish Airports Director and the Directors of Engineering, Commercial Development, Finance, Personnel, Public Affairs and Planning; together with the Solicitor and the Inspector of Airside Safety and Operations (see Appendix 3.2). The Executive normally meets monthly and is responsible for management of the Authority's airports within the framework of approved policies, for development and presentation of strategic policy and major capital expenditure proposals and for the national and international representation of the Authority.

3.26. The position of Commercial Development Director has been recently introduced with the objective of identifying, developing and promoting commercial opportunities in all non-traffic fields to enhance BAA's profitability. With the establishment of the Trading Department in February 1984 he now has reporting to him the Trading Marketing Manager, the Trading General Manager and the Trading Information Management Manager, as well as the Air Cargo Manager and the General Manager Property (see Appendix 3.3).

[1]See Appendix 3.2 for an organisation chart.

3.27. In broad terms the Commercial Development Director and his organisation are responsible for the establishment of policy for property, cargo and all the activities known within BAA as 'Trading'. Trading includes the direction of retail operations, the duty-free and tax-free shops, and the letting of concessions for them and their pricing policies; the identification of new products and services, tendering, merchandising, promotion and advertising; and the management of the contractual relationship with the concessionaires. A more detailed description of the responsibilities of the Trading Department is to be found at paragraph 5.37.

3.28. The Airport Directors have 'line' (including budget) responsibility for all the traffic and commercial activities at their airports. Amongst those reporting to the Director for Heathrow is the Deputy Director Terminals, who in turn has a General Manager responsible for each Terminal. Similarly the Director Gatwick/Stansted[1] has at Gatwick a Deputy Director, with a Terminal General Manager and a Property and Commercial Manager; and at Stansted there is a General Manager with managers responsible for commercial and property matters. Similar arrangements prevail at the Scottish airports. The Commercial Development Director is available in a 'staff' capacity to advise airport managements.

3.29. Thus BAA has, within the area covered by our terms of reference, a separate specialist organisation dealing with commercial development, under its own Director; however, those staff at each airport who are involved in implementing commercial policy do not report to him but direct to airport management.

---

[1] Following the Government decision to develop Stansted (see paragraph 3.15) the separate post of Director of Stansted was established from 1 September 1985.

C

CHAPTER 4

BAA commercial activities

4.1. Commercial activities, as defined in our reference, fall into three categories:

(*a*) provision of goods and services to the public;

(*b*) provision of services to airlines; and

(*c*) leases and property administration.

The first two are limited to provision by third parties under arrangements made by BAA.

Provision of goods and services to the public

4.2. The major part of BAA's commercial revenue is derived from this service—nearly £120 million in 1984–85. As noted in paragraph 3.21 it is the general policy of the Authority to provide for the sale of goods and services to the public at its airports by means of concession arrangements with private enterprise companies. The Authority provides the premises, fitted out for their intended use. The concessionaire is not required to pay rent or rates, but pays a percentage of turnover to the Authority: the concessionaire also pays for specific services. Concessions are let by competitive tender, and normally run for five years, providing for regular testing of the market.

4.3. The principal concessions for the supply of goods to the public are:

Duty-free and tax-free shops. These are situated on the 'airside' of the airport (ie that area accessible only to passengers with boarding cards) usually in International Departure Lounges. They are available only to passengers departing on international flights and flights to the Republic of Ireland and the Channel Islands; they are not available to arriving passengers or passengers departing on domestic flights, and they must be operated under Customs control.

Bookshops and gift shops. These are retail shops which, although operated by concessionaires, now trade under the BAA brand name of 'Skyshop' (the name of the airport is also used on some BAA own brand gift items on sale); this concept was introduced in 1981–82. The first Skyshop was opened at Gatwick in spring 1983, and all have now been renamed and refurbished with the exception of one shop in Terminal 1 at Heathrow which will be converted shortly. They are provided in Departures and Arrivals concourses (on the landside of the airports) and in International Departure Lounges.

Other retail shops. A number of specialist shops have been opened recently: these trade under the name of the concessionaire and, in some cases, the concessionaire will be responsible for special fittings required for his business.

Catering. There is a varying range both air- and landside of self-service buffets, bars and restaurants, although the perceived trend of public demand is increasingly towards self-service snacks and away from full meals with restaurant service. The caterer not only has to meet the normal requirements of passengers and others during the hours the airport is open (usually at least 18 hours a day) but must be prepared to deal with the large and sudden demands that arise when aircraft are unexpectedly delayed or diverted. The Authority provides the public eating area and the back-up kitchens and preparation areas, with all fixed or heavy catering equipment. The caterer provides all loose items. Because of space limitations in all the terminal buildings now operating it is not practicable to provide the full range of kitchen, preparation and ancillary areas needed for more than one concessionaire. Catering is therefore generally the subject of a single concession to cover the whole of the catering in a terminal building. However, small single-purpose outlets (ice cream, for example) are completely self-contained and do not depend on the main catering facilities.

4.4. Because concessionaires are not generally subject to the stimulus of direct competition—and in most cases BAA regards it as impracticable because of limitations of space to have competing concessionaires offering the same product range in the same area—the Authority through the concession agreement specifies the range of goods to be provided. Some control is also exercised over prices. The Authority also carries out checks intended to ensure that the quality, both of the goods and of the retailer's service, is maintained.

4.5. In addition to arrangements for the supply of goods to the public, BAA makes arrangements for the public to have access to a number of services which are in general demand by travellers. The most important of these are:

Car rental. Desk space for up to four concessionaires is provided in each Arrivals concourse: in most cases the Authority also provides separate back-up parking and ancillary accommodation.

Flight insurance. Desk accommodation is provided in the airside Departure Lounges in Terminals 1, 2 and 3 at Heathrow, and at Gatwick. Some banks in landside Departure concourses also provide flight insurance.

Car parking. Provision is made for both short- and long-term parking. Most car parks are the subject of a concession agreement. The exceptions are Heathrow, Stansted and Glasgow. Heathrow is operated under a management contract under which the manager is paid his costs plus a management fee, all revenues accruing to the Authority. Stansted is operated directly by BAA. Glasgow is let to NCP on an exclusive 99-year lease agreed several years before the airport was taken over by BAA.

Banking. Facilities are provided in landside Arrivals and Departures concourses. Payment to the Authority is based either on turnover or on the number of passengers passing through the terminal. The only exception is one bank occupying premises at a fixed rent under a time-expired lease: in this case a new arrangement is being negotiated.

Petrol filling stations. These are provided at Heathrow, Gatwick and Glasgow under a variety of financial arrangements.

Hotel bookings. Desk accommodation is provided on landside Arrivals concourses.

Advertising. Sites are let under an agency contract.

27

Provision of services to airlines

4.6. These services are collectively known as ' ground handling services '. The principal services are:

Passenger handling; from check-in to embarkation, or from disembarkation to baggage reclaim, or to re-embarkation for transferring passengers.

Baggage handling.

Cargo handling.

Aircraft technical handling. Maintenance and repair and towing of aircraft.

Ancillary handling. Other miscellaneous services including:

Flight catering

Aircraft cleaning

Crew transport

Passenger coaching

Disabled passenger services

Aircraft security

4.7. Ground handling services are mainly carried out by airlines, although some specialist companies are also involved, particularly in respect of the ancillary handling services. It is the policy of the Authority, in order to avoid wasteful duplication of facilities and under-utilisation of space, to restrict the numbers of airlines and others having the right to provide handling services. Those airlines which have not been granted this right buy in the necessary service from another airline or handling agent. This policy of restriction is not fully applied at Heathrow, mainly because of rights which had been established before the Authority was set up. Eight airlines there have long-established rights to provide all the handling services set out in paragraph 4.6, both for themselves and to other airlines (except that they may not provide passenger or baggage handling services in a terminal not used by their own air services);[1] a further 19 are permitted to check in their own passengers and 17 are allowed to handle their own cargo.

4.8. In most cases ground handling rights are not themselves the subject of a licence, but the Authority derives rents from leasing or licensing the accommodation used, which can range from a check-in desk through storage areas for handling equipment to a complete cargo hangar. In some cases, particularly when an off-airport operator provides an ancillary handling service, the right to trade on the airport is directly the subject of a licence and the Authority receives a percentage of the revenue being earned.

---

[1]There are two exceptions to this general rule. British Airways (then British European Airways) carried out handling for other airlines in Terminal 2 at the time when all short-haul services were concentrated in that terminal. When all British European Airways services were moved to Terminal 1, BEA continued to provide handling services to other airlines in Terminal 2, and BA still does so. The second exception is Aer Lingus, which under its contract with BAA as ' handler of last resort ' (see paragraph 11.48) has the right to provide services in any terminal, although at present its activities are confined to Terminal 1 (used by its own services) and some baggage handling at Terminal 3.

Air traffic services (ATS)

4.9. The background to the supply of ATS at BAA airports may for convenience be taken from paragraphs 7.3 to 7.6 of our 1983 report 'Civil Aviation Authority'.[1]

7.3. ATS is provided by the (CAA) at all the BAA airports, that is Heathrow, Gatwick, Stansted, Glasgow, Edinburgh, Prestwick and Aberdeen. BAA told us that it believed it was precluded by section 2(1) of the Airports Authority Act 1975 from providing these services itself, or obtaining them from other suppliers, without the consent of the Secretary of State. The Act states:

> It shall be the duty of the (BAA) to provide at its aerodromes such services and facilities as are in its opinion necessary or desirable for their operation, but the (BAA) shall not provide any navigation services except with the consent in writing of the Secretary of State (section 2(1), Airports Authority Act 1975).

7.4. The provision by the (CAA) of ATS at BAA airports is in accordance with the Civil Aviation Act 1982:

> It shall be the duty of the CAA to provide air navigation services . . . in the United Kingdom . . . to the extent to which it appears to the CAA that such services are necessary and are not being provided by it (either alone or jointly with another person) or by some other person (section 72(1), Civil Aviation Act 1982).

> There is no contract between the (CAA) and BAA governing the provision of these services.

7.5. BAA told us that from time to time it did consider seeking Ministerial consent to change the position but had reached no positive view. One factor which had influenced it was the high standard of service provided by the (CAA).

7.6. BAA was nevertheless concerned about the level of costs incurred by the (CAA) in the provision of the services at its airports, because these formed part of the costs borne by their users and influenced the acceptability of its airports. It had suggested to the (CAA) that a joint body be formed to discuss matters concerning the costs and charges which had an impact on the acceptability of its airports, but the (CAA) rejected the idea.

4.10. BAA told us that it considered the wording of the 1975 Act permits an approach to the Secretary of State if a change in the ATS arrangements is thought desirable; and that examples outside BAA showed that considerable savings could be made if other options became available. The Authority had not approached the Secretary of State for consent to consider the provision of ATS by a private sector contractor because for some years it was not convinced that an alternative service was available in the United Kingdom of the same high standard as that provided by the CAA. The Authority now recognised that other contractors provide a satisfactory standard of ATS in the UK; nevertheless the Authority thought it 'would be very difficult indeed to introduce a contractor other than the Civil Aviation Authority in the London Area'. BAA agreed that this would not apply to its smaller airports.

[1]Cmnd 9068. Where we have placed the letters CAA or BAA in brackets in this quotation this indicates that in the original text the word 'Authority' was used, which would be confusing in the present context.

Leases and property administration

4.11. The concessions and licences described in paragraphs 4.2 to 4.8 usually involve granting to the concessionaire or licensee the right to use land and buildings (or space in a building), under arrangements to which the provisions of Part II of the Landlord and Tenant Act 1954 do not apply.[1] Other land and buildings are let under different arrangements: land upon which tenants erect their own buildings (such as a hotel) is let by ground lease: other land and buildings or parts of buildings are let at rack rents by lease or short-term tenancy. In some cases in addition to the rent the Authority receives a payment reflecting the volume of business being done. Rents and services produced an income of nearly £60 million in 1984–85.

4.12. BAA's 'user' clauses and sub-letting provisions tend to be restrictive in order to enable the Authority to retain overall control of the operation of its airports. It is the Authority's policy generally to restrict lettings to airport-related uses, but some relaxation of this policy has been necessary when there is a surplus of accommodation (eg at Prestwick).

Importance of revenue from commercial services

4.13. The significance of the Authority's revenue from commercial services can be readily appreciated from Table 4.1.

TABLE 4.1 **BAA income and expenditure, 1984–5**

	Commercial services		Traffic services		Total	
	£m	%	£m	%	£m	%
Income	179·0	49·5	182·6	50·5	361·6	100
Expenditure	82·7	28·8	204·3	71·2	287·0	100
Profit or loss	96·3		(21·7)		74·6	

Source: BAA Annual Report and Accounts 1984–85, page 56. No allowance is made for the charge of £2·6 million on account of asset life revisions, which has not been allocated to activities. See Annual Report and Accounts 1984–85, page 49, note 3.9.

Even after making allowance for the difficulty of allocating expenditure to commercial services[2] it is clear that without the revenue from these services the Authority would be likely to be in deficit (or much higher traffic charges would be required). The Authority certainly does not think it would have been able—as has been the case—to fund a steadily increasing capital expenditure programme almost entirely from its own resources, thus avoiding a considerable burden of servicing capital borrowings.

4.14. The Authority's policy for its commercial activities is most recently set out in the Annual Report and Accounts 1984–85:

Of the facilities and services provided at airports, some are unique to the airport environment, such as ground handling of aircraft and air traffic control, whereas others, such as shops and car parks, are common throughout

---

[1] Under these provisions (which do not apply in Scotland) an occupant of property has a right to continued occupation, subject to determination by the Courts, after the contractual term of the occupation has expired.

[2] The problems of attributing general costs to specific activities are discussed in Chapter 7 and our conclusions are set out in paragraph 7.60.

30

the land. Since its formation in 1965 it has been BAA policy that the latter services should, wherever possible, be provided by specialist companies, with the BAA providing essential airport services and facilities.

BAA is committed to the concept of maximum development of income from sources other than aircraft landing and parking fees and will aim to maximise profit in its commercial affairs, consistent with the need to maintain the credibility of its pricing structures on a long term basis and with its obligations as a public enterprise.

The major revenue earners are from Duty- and Tax-Free Trading. This will continue to be so. Actual penetration levels are such as to indicate the availability of further growth potential and this will be addessed in particular by stronger efforts to communicate the retail price advantage of duty-free and also efforts to persuade non-buyers in the departure lounges to visit the shops.

Whilst the main core of the business will continue to be the traditional Duty-Free area, strong emphasis will also now be given to other areas. Overall, however, the greater part of medium term growth is seen as more likely to derive from increasing market penetration than from encouraging increases in average spend.

The approach towards catering on airports has been the subject of considerable innovation in a persistent endeavour to develop this activity. A heavy emphasis will be put on the identification of consumer needs, enhancement of design, flexibility, and satisfaction of market trends through improving quality, value and particularly service to customers.

4.15. Measurement of the Authority's performance in the realisation of this policy is not easy. Table 4.2 sets out BAA's income from commercial activities. The figures show that there has been a six-fold increase in revenue from commercial activities from 1974–75 to 1984–85: much of this is accounted for by inflation, or by the increased number of passengers. In an endeavour to provide objective measures of its performance discounting external influences, the Authority has developed a number of performance indicators and has carried out some comparative studies. We deal with these in turn.

4.16. Certain indicators are published in the Annual Report and Accounts 1984–85. Of one group of three indicators[1] the Authority says:

They are not affected by changes in accounting philosophy, in particular depreciation, and so in combination, are a good measure of performance.[2]

However, the Authority told us that these indicators were primarily developed as information for the reader of the Annual Report: the Authority does not use indicators of this kind to assess its commercial performance.

4.17. The Authority uses overall income or income per passenger (both at constant prices) for budgeting, target-setting and forecasting. In practice, only the past three years are considered by the Authority: forecasts are made up to five years ahead. BAA has reservations about using these measures as indicators in many applications, for two main reasons:

---

[1]Income per passenger; expenditure before depreciation per passenger; trading profit before depreciation per passenger.

[2]BAA Annual Report and Accounts 1984–85, page 58.

(*a*) lack of space in terminals means that as passenger numbers increase congestion problems will reduce the attractiveness of individual facilities; and

(*b*) passenger behaviour is not uniform. Differences in, for example, nationality, age, income, destination and journey purpose may have major influences on consumption patterns at airports. As an illustrative example passengers travelling from Terminal 1 to Norway spend on average £10·56 on duty-free while those going to Amsterdam spend only £2·90.

4.18. At our request BAA has provided some more detailed indicators, covering the past ten years and concentrating on the commercial activities which are the subject of our inquiry. Table 4.3 gives in lines 1 and 2 the income and trading profit per passenger indices from the Annual Report[1] converted to a base year figure of 1979–80.[2] Lines 3 to 8 in that table are disaggregations produced by the Authority at our request.

4.19. Lines 1 and 2 in Table 4.3 show the rise and fall in income and profit per passenger from all BAA activities at constant prices. They are an attempt to adjust the figures to reduce two major sources of difficulty in the year-by-year comparisons; the growth in passengers and inflation. However, the picture presented by these figures is distorted, particularly by:

(*a*) sharp rises in landing and aircraft parking fees, firstly in 1978 following the Authority's assumption of responsibility for security, and secondly in 1980 in response to EFL constraints imposed by Government; and

(*b*) the inclusion of rents and services to tenants, which do not move in a direct relationship with changes in the numbers of passengers.

Lines 3 and 4 cover the rise and fall in income and profit per passenger from all commercial activities, and are intended to eliminate the distortion resulting from (*a*). Lines 5 and 6 cover the rise and fall in income and profit per passenger from concessions, and are intended to eliminate the distortion resulting from (*b*). Finally, lines 7 and 8 cover the rise and fall in income and profit per international departing passenger (IDP) from concessions, and are intended to give greater weight to the effect of changes in the numbers of those passengers who have access to duty- and tax-free shops. All eight lines from Table 4.3 are reproduced in graphic form in Figure 4.1, and Table 4.4 shows the average annual movements in percentages; from these the general picture may be more easily appreciated. There is considerable movement both up and down in all the indices: the reversals occur roughly at the same time for each indicator and therefore probably show the effects of causes which have not been precisely identified.

4.20. Commenting on these figures the Authority told us that the analysis of the influence of individual factors affecting commercial performance has always been an extremely difficult one, both in terms of measurement and in determining which factors represent underlying causes and which are merely intermediate variables. The Authority believes that attempts to find simple explanations for complex phenomena should be treated with extreme caution.

---

[1] BAA Annual Report and Accounts 1984–85, page 58, lines (4) and (6).

[2] Because a detailed breakdown of profit is not available for earlier years, all the figures are calculated in relation to a base year of 1979–80 = 100 in order to produce comparability.

TABLE 4.3. **Performance indicators** (Base 1979–80 = 100)

All indices calculated at constant prices

	Actuals											Forecast (based on budgets)					See Table 4·2 Line
	1974–75	1975–76	1976–77	1977–78	1978–79	1979–80	1980–81	1981–82	1982–83	1983–84	1984–85	1985–86	1986–87	1987–88	1988–89	1989–90	
(1) Total income per passenger	91·32	92·17	97·02	101·00	105·71	100·0	115·70	112·23	106·14	107·16	105·43	*	*	*	*	*	6
(2) Total profit (before depreciation) per passenger	101·88	103·69	128·03	130·84	112·97	100·0	128·80	123·81	117·44	126·44	138·48	*	*	*	*	*	7
(3) Commercial income per passenger	105·42	99·60	104·14	110·83	104·10	100·0	100·21	102·41	106·32	109·52	112·70	[Figures omitted. See note on page iv.]					8
(4) Commercial profit per passenger†	*	*	105·90	123·48	106·56	100·0	103·81	107·72	128·56	143·22	152·36	*	*	*	*	*	9
(5) Concession income per passenger	98·34	94·51	105·55	110·81	106·36	100·0	99·98	101·12	106·17	112·67	116·31	[Figures omitted. See note on page iv.]					10
(6) Concession profit per passenger†	*	*	*	*	*	100·0	97·26	98·55	106·93	115·61	117·30	*	*	*	*	*	11
(7) Concession income per IDP	91·47	95·16	106·74	107·63	104·80	100·0	97·45	98·74	104·18	111·44	113·89	[Figures omitted. See note on page iv.]					12
(8) Concession profit per IDP†	*	*	*	*	*	100·0	94·80	96·24	104·93	114·35	114·85	*	*	*	*	*	13

Source: BAA special study for MMC.

*Not available. †After CCA depreciation.

35

TABLE 4.4 **BAA income and profit: past and projected rate of change**
% annual rate of growth (decline)

| | | AT CONSTANT PRICES | | | | |
| | | ACTUAL | | | PROJECTED (BUDGET) | per cent |
	10 years 1974–75 to 1984–85	3 years 1974–75 to 1977–78	3 years 1977–78 to 1980–81	4 years 1980–81 to 1984–85	5 years 1984–85 to 1989–90	See Table 4.2 Line
1. Total income per passenger	1·4	3·4	4·6	(2·3)	*	6
2. Total profit per passenger	3·0	8·7	(0·6)	1·7	*	7
3. Commercial income per passenger	1·0	1·7	(3·3)	3·8	[†]	8
4. Commercial profit per passenger	4·7[a]	16·6[b]	(5·6)	10·1	*	9
5. Concession income per passenger	1·7	4·1	(3·4)	3·9	[†]	10
6. Concession profit per passenger	3·2[c]	*	(2·7)[d]	4·8	*	11
7. Concession income per IDP	2·2	5·6	(3·3)	4·0	[†]	12
8. Concession profit per IDP	2·8[c]	*	(5·2)[d]	4·9	*	13
9. Total passengers	6·5	8·8	6·8	4·5	[†]	14
10. Total IDP	5·9	7·2	6·6	4·4	[†]	15

Source: BAA special study for MMC.

[a] 8 years 1976–77 to 1984–85 only.
[b] 1 year 1976–77 to 1977–78 only.
[c] 5 years 1979–80 to 1984–85 only.
[d] 1 year 1979–80 to 1980–81 only.

11. United Kingdom consumers' expenditure per capita	1·43	(0·25)	3·09	1·47	*	

*Not available.
†Figures omitted. See note on page iv.
Source: CSO economic trends.

4.21. The Authority says that, broadly speaking, the factors which might account for the changes observed are of two kinds: extrinsic, which are changes in economic and social factors which are outside its control, and intrinsic, which relate to the performance of BAA and concessionaires.

4.22. Amongst the extrinsic factors which the Authority has considered are:

(a) inflation;

(b) growth in United Kingdom consumer expenditure;

(c) performance of overseas economies;

(d) growth in passenger numbers;

(e) exchange rate fluctuations;

(f) changes in proportion of international passengers;

(g) changes in taxation;

(h) changes in passenger type;

(i) competition from other sources;

(j) global changes in consumer taste (eg from dark to light spirits and away from tobacco);

(k) airline performance;

(l) air traffic delays;

(m) absolute price;

(n) price relative to alternative suppliers (eg United Kingdom and foreign High Streets, other duty-free shops and airlines); and

(o) propensity to spend.

Most of these can be measured in one form or another though there remain important technical problems in attempting to relate them to BAA's performance as shown in the tables.

4.23. Intrinsic factors, though sometimes more easy to recognise, tend to be harder to quantify. Amongst those considered by the Authority are:

(a) concessionaire performance;

(b) major redevelopments of terminals;

(c) promotional activities;

(d) changes in individual shop design or layout;

(e) contractual changes;

(f) introduction of new product lines;

(g) space allocated to commercial activities;

(h) congestion in terminals and in individual shops;

(i) terminal operational policies;

(j) advertising;

(k) design; and

(l) staff training and motivation.

-4.24. The Authority told us that although all these effects (both intrinsic and extrinsic) have clearly been operating it had not found it possible to demonstrate incontrovertibly which were affecting its performance to a significant extent, let alone the magnitude of their relative effects. More generally, it has not found it possible to isolate the changes caused by extrinsic factors from those which have been caused internally. Despite repeated attempts in the past, BAA has been unable to produce a consistently satisfactory model which explains and predicts commercial performance.

4.25. As a result of these problems, the Authority has found it impossible to distinguish between a variety of plausible (though possibly contradictory) explanations of its commercial performance over the time period. It cannot, therefore, offer a single definitive account of the fluctuations shown.

Comparative studies—rents

4.26. In mid–1983 the Authority carried out a study of its performance in relation to property management by comparing rents at Heathrow with the index of off-airport rents published regularly by Hillier Parker May and Rowden in conjunction with the Investors Chronicle (ICHP), and with the movements in the retail price index (RPI) and new construction costs (CNC). The Authority tells us that the results show that for all the categories of property considered:

(a) Heathrow has out-performed the ICHP Index;

(b) Heathrow warehouse rents have equalled or exceeded the RPI and CNC Index, but some Heathrow offices in common with national trends have not done so.

BAA, like other landlords in England, is constrained by the provisions of Part II of the Landlord and Tenant Act 1954 (but see paragraph 4.11). A further constraint is that the Authority on its formation inherited a number of long-term leases on terms which do not provide for rents to be reviewed to market value as has been conventional for a number of years.

Comparative studies—overall performance

4.27. The Authority has also carried out studies to compare overall performance at its airports with performance at other similar airports. One such study compared the BAA's Scottish airports with published data on the ten largest British local authority airports.[1] Because available data were not strictly comparable, a number of adjustments had to be made, involving a degree of estimation. Those of the Authority's conclusions which are relevant to our inquiry are therefore reproduced here only in general form:

(a) BAA Scottish airports perform well in respect of income, with similar levels of landing fees but with greater success in the generation of commercial income.

(b) Profitability of the BAA Scottish airports is lower on a per passenger basis than at the local authority airports, because the latter have a higher proportion of international passengers ie those with access to duty- and tax-free shops. When a like-for-like comparison is made, BAA's return on

---

[1]Birmingham, Bristol, Cardiff, East Midlands, Leeds/Bradford, Liverpool, Luton, Manchester, Newcastle and Teesside.

capital employed is superior to the equivalent estimated return for local authority airports.

4.28. A second study compared overall performance of the Authority's South-East airports[1] with similar continental airports.[2] As a result of that study first carried out on financial information for 1980 and last updated using 1983 accounts the Authority has concluded that:

(a) The proportion of total income derived from commercial activity was the same for the BAA airports as for the European airports (55 per cent).

(b) The European airports derived two-thirds of their non-traffic income from rents and the remainder from concessions: for the BAA airports these proportions were reversed. The concession income per passenger at the European airports was half that of BAA;[3] the total non-traffic income per passenger at the European airports was, however, some 8 per cent higher than at the BAA airports (using exchange rates derived from a recent OECD study of purchasing power parities in order to eliminate possible distortion arising from using market exchange rates).

(c) Overall the European airports had higher costs and revenues per passenger and were considerably less profitable; this was reflected in a much higher level of debt (and servicing charges) incurred to finance capital expenditure.

4.29. Because of the limitations of the available data neither of these studies can do more than suggest that the BAA airports, when compared with similar airports in the United Kingdom or on the Continent, are performing well in relation to their commercial activities.

Conclusions and recommendations

(a) Air Traffic Services

4.30. While it might be difficult to introduce another contractor for the supply of ATS to replace the CAA in the London area, we recommend, in view of the potential reduction in costs to airlines, that the Authority should consider the possibility of employing another contractor at its smaller airports.

(b) Commercial activities generally

4.31. It is clear that none of the available statistics provides, on its own, a conclusive indication of the level of performance achieved by the Authority in its commercial activities. The evidence of satisfactory performance is most persuasive in relation to rents, where some comparison with the outside property market has been attempted. We discuss rents and property in more detail in Chapter 10. So far as concessions are concerned, interpretation of the figures is subject to two major difficulties:

(a) Comparisons are internal over time, or external with airports elsewhere. No 'absolute' measures are attempted, and it is difficult to see how

---

[1] Heathrow, Gatwick and Stansted.

[2] The airports of Paris (taking them as one system), Frankfurt and Schiphol (Amsterdam).

[3] For a possible explanation see the comparative figures for international passengers in Appendix 3.1.

comparison with more normal markets would be possible. Thus the figures are equally compatible with:

> (i) a slow and generally unsatisfactory rate of improvement in performance from an inadequate base;
>
> (ii) a slow and generally very satisfactory rate of improvement in performance from a high base;
> or any intermediate position.

(b) The nature and effect of external influences remain obscure. Looking only at the most recent few years, there is a temptation to ascribe the marked improvement over those years to recent BAA initiatives and concentration on commercial activities. But a similar upturn occurred between 1974 and 1976 (when no special initiatives by BAA were brought to our notice) and this was followed by an equally marked downturn (with, again, no specific evidence of this being caused by any deterioration in BAA performance) (see Table 4.4).

4.32. The Authority told us that:

> taken in itself, a 2 per cent real growth per year on a per passenger basis with no increase in market share and no technological improvements appears a commendable ten-year performance, particularly when the problems involved in managing the very rapid increase in passengers are taken into account.

We do not think it safe to draw any inference from the figures which is not supported by the more detailed examination of the Authority's commercial activities contained in the following chapters.

4.33. We recognise that the Authority has already made considerable efforts to measure its performance. Nevertheless, some of the material presented in this chapter had not previously been examined by the Authority in this form. We recommend that the Authority should try to develop measures which give clearer indications of performance in its commercial activities. In particular we recommend that efforts should be made to produce specific indicators, dealing separately with such items as duty-free liquor, tobacco products, catering, car parks etc. Such disaggregation would, we think, make it easier to assess the effects of the various factors set out in paragraphs 4.22 and 4.23. It would also facilitate the use, where appropriate, of inflation indices specific to the product concerned instead of a blanket application of the RPI.

CHAPTER 5

BAA organisation and planning

The Board, corporate strategy and formal planning

The Board

5.1. The composition and activities of BAA's main Board have been outlined in paragraphs 3.23 and 3.24. BAA's Chairman told us that the ways in which the Board considers commercial matters include:

(a) discussion of a quarterly report on commercial performance;

(b) determining pricing policy;

(c) presentations to the Board by the Commercial Development Director. The most recent presentation was in January 1984. No date had been set for the next presentation; and

(d) inclusion in each Board agenda of a 'Members' Items' provision.

5.2. Examples of matters covered by reports are given in paragraph 6.1 *et seq*.

5.3. Examination of BAA's Board minutes for the period April 1983 to April 1985 showed that the following matters relevant to commercial activities were raised under 'Members' Items':

(a) signposting of the Heathrow Business Centre;

(b) British Midland Airways: self-handling at Heathrow;

(c) possible reference of BAA's duty- and tax-free activities to the Office of Fair Trading;

(d) the low level of duty- and tax-free sales at Gatwick;

(e) taxis at Gatwick; and

(f) telephone facilities at terminals.

5.4. At a meeting with two of BAA's non-executive directors we were told that, in addition to discussions of commercial matters at Board meetings, there is regular contact between non-executive directors and commercial/trading staff.

5.5. Non-executive members of the Board are not allocated specific functional responsibilities. There is thus no member with particular responsibility for commercial matters. BAA told us that the Board had considered a study carried out in November 1981 by the Central Policy Review Staff in which it was recommended that functional responsibilities should be assigned to non-executive members. The Board had decided against such a system: it deliberately 'did not want to second-guess management'.

5.6. As we note in paragraphs 5.30 to 5.32 part-time members of the Board are encouraged to take an informal interest in areas of BAA's activities according to their particular expertise. Two non-executive members of the present Board have

43

a commercial/industrial background. A former member was a director of a chain of retail stores. There is at present no member with retailing experience. A part-time member chairs the Board's Audit Committee.

5.7. It is the Board's view that any conflict between commercial and airport management should preferably be resolved at airport level. Thus the Board does not seek to lay down general guidelines as to how to arrive at 'trade-offs' amongst a variety of objectives. But the Board does intervene in specific instances. A recent (April 1984) example of Board intervention in commercial matters was the decision that the duty- and tax-free shop in the redeveloped Terminal 3 at Heathrow airport should not face passengers directly after they had passed through security checks, but should be set off to the left-hand side.

5.8. Another example in 1984 of Board involvement in commercial matters concerned on-airport advertising for cigarettes. The Board had decided in 1975 that advertising for cigarettes would be permitted only close to, at the entrance to or inside duty-free shops which sold cigarettes. The Executive in 1984 suggested that a significant increase in duty-free sales could result from more extensive advertising at airports. The Board rejected the proposal.

Formal planning

5.9. BAA's objectives have been stated in its Corporate Plan since 1976 and, as part of a review of all nationalised industries, were formally agreed with the Government in 1982. In the 1985 Corporate Plan the objectives are as follows:

The Authority's primary objective is to respond to the present and future needs of air transport in an efficient and profitable way by operating, planning and developing its airports so that air travellers and cargo may pass through safely, swiftly and as conveniently as possible.

In support of this overall objective, the essential policies are:

—To maintain, using the regulatory framework, high standards of safety for aircraft, passengers and airport staff, and to ensure that these standards match development in the air transport industry.

—To ensure, within the limits of the Authority's powers, high standards of security against terrorism and crime in its airports.

—To provide facilities at the airports such as are necessary to enable them to meet the needs of air transport in a safe and cost-effective manner.

—To improve operating efficiency and to ensure as far as possible that it meets the financial and performance aims, external financing limits and other targets agreed with the Government from time to time.

—To meet the needs of airport users for the provision of goods and services in such a way as to encourage a competitive and commercial approach and to ensure the effective utilisation of its assets and opportunities.

—To improve, as far as its powers permit, the range and quality not only of services offered to its customers, but also those provided by other organisations and to have regard to the best practice of other airport authorities in the UK and abroad.

—To develop and uphold a high standard of design in every aspect which is cost-effective and visually and functionally appropriate.

—To ensure, as a good employer, fair pay and conditions of service for employees and to encourage a working partnership leading to higher productivity and higher standards of service to the public through proper arrangements for participation, consultation and negotiation.

—To operate in harmony with the communities adjoining its airports and to seek to maintain a balance of interest between those communities and the needs of air transport through the provision of adequate facilities for consultation.

—To market its skills and experience in its own specialist field both in its own right and in support of the efforts of other British consultants, contractors and suppliers in the service of the air transport industry.

Most of these essential policies are largely unaltered from the original (1976) statement of 'essential priorities'. The design policy was added in 1984. The commercial policy was reworded in 1985; in the 1984 Corporate Plan it was: 'To maintain, as a public enterprise, a competitive and commercial approach to its operations, and to improve operating efficiency.'

5.10. At its March 1985 meeting the Board recommended that the order of the 'essential policies' as shown in the Corporate Plan should be rearranged to give higher implicit priority to statements concerning facilities and services. The order in which essential policies are listed in paragraph 5.9 results from that decision.

5.11. The commercial policy section of the 1985 Corporate Plan is reproduced at Appendix 5.1. The commercial strategy section is reproduced at Appendix 5.2. The policy section includes the statement that:

BAA is committed to the concept of maximum development of income from sources other than aircraft landing and parking fees and will aim to maximise profit in its commercial affairs, consistent with the need to maintain the credibility of its pricing structures on a long-term basis and with its obligations as a public enterprise.

5.12. In addition to the objectives, the Corporate Planning process involves targets (and also forecasts of air traffic). Items covered by the targets agreed with the Government (see paragraph 7.7) are:

(a) rate of return on net assets;

(b) costs, excluding depreciation, per passenger;

(c) passengers per payroll hour; and

(d) 'Scottish Airports break even'.

5.13. The targets agreed each year between the Board and the Managing Director include the four 'Government targets' plus six others. These are (with the targets for 1985–86 in brackets):

(e) to increase duty- and tax-free income per international departing passenger by x per cent (4·75 per cent in real terms);

(f) to increase other concession income (excluding duty- and tax-free and car parking) per passenger by x per cent (4·5 per cent in real terms);

(g) to increase gross rental income by x per cent (4·5 per cent in real terms);

45

(*h*) to increase passengers per £1,000 of staff costs by x per cent (no increase in 1985–86 over previous year);

(*i*) to reduce the number of complaints per 100,000 passengers to below 12; and

(*j*) to achieve availability of 'passenger-sensitive' mechanical equipment, such as lifts, escalators and travellators, of 96 per cent.

5.14. Targets, in addition to those agreed with the Government, were introduced for 1983–84. At its meeting in January 1984 the Board agreed that:

(*a*) 'Targets should be set annually in the light of the latest available information rather than on the performance originally targeted or achieved for this year.'

(*b*) 'Targets should normally be set for a one year period only. This allows the targets to take better account of the opportunities and threats facing the BAA. Targets which fail to do this will inevitably lose credibility. One year targeting is also consistent with the detailed budgeting process.'

(*c*) 'Targets should normally be set at more onerous levels than those adopted for budgeting purposes.'

5.15. The Board considers targets on two separate occasions within the planning cycle. Provisional targets are set in May or June for the year which will commence in the following April. In the following March or April the Board confirms or modifies the targets.

5.16. At its March 1984 meeting the Board decided that the 1984–85 targets for duty- and tax-free income per international departing passenger (IDP) and other commercial income per terminal passenger should be increased (from 7·0 to 7·5 per cent and from 2·0 to 3·5 per cent in real terms respectively) from the provisional targets previously set and that no change should be made to the rental income target.

5.17. The paper presented to the Board for discussion of targets states the three targets: duty- and tax-free income per IDP, other commercial income per terminal passenger, and gross rental income. In commenting on these figures the paper may note, for example, a particular effort to be made in tax-free goods. Beyond this no further detail is supplied.

5.18. If a Board member wishes to consider how any target has been made up, he or she can question the Managing Director, or make comparison with the budget figures previously or concurrently being agreed. The budget contains figures for the last year and the forecast for the next five years. The level of detail for the current year is:

Duty- and tax-free:	liquor, tobacco, tax-free
Duty-paid:	Skyshops, other duty-paid goods
Catering	
Car parks:	short-term, long-term
'Arrivals':	car rental, banking
In-flight catering	

5.19. Within the planning cycle which starts in May or June and ends in March or April of the following year, detailed objectives are agreed for the Marketing Plan, by terminal and by, for example, trading product group and sub-group. The degree of detail is as follows:

Product group	Sub-groups
Tax-free	Perfume, clothing, photographic and electrical goods, watches and jewellery, gifts.
Tax-paid	Books, newspapers and magazines, confectionery, other merchandise.

5.20. Details of the objectives for product groups and sub-groups are available to Board members if they ask for them.

5.21. For target-setting as a whole the principle is that targets cascade downwards through the organisation so that those agreed at higher levels are reflected in those agreed at lower levels, although they may not agree precisely in arithmetical terms. For example, the Managing Director may agree a target of a 4 per cent increase in rental income with the Board and may then agree targets of 5 per cent with the Director, Heathrow, 3 per cent with the Director, Scottish Airports, and 3·5 per cent with the Directors, Gatwick and Stansted.

5.22. An additional complexity arises in the case of commercial activities. As explained above, targets are initially agreed between the BAA Board and the Managing Director, who then agrees airport targets with the Airport Directors, and an overall commercial target with the Commercial Development Director. Because these targets are agreed, rather than imposed, there are likely to be minor discrepancies between them. The Commercial Development Director may also be prepared to adopt a more optimistic approach than the Airport Directors. For example, in comparison with the 1985–86 targets agreed between the Managing Director and the Board (paragraph 5.13), the Commercial Development Director accepted higher targets for duty- and tax-free income and rental income, but a slightly lower target for other concession income.

5.23. The process of corporate planning in BAA is summarised at Appendix 5.3. The process includes the preparation of a Business Plan for each airport.

5.24. As Appendix 5.3 shows, BAA uses the Corporate Plan as a primary means of communicating not only with the Government but also with its employees, the unions and, in the form of 'Policies and Programs', with the airlines and other air transport customers.

Physical planning

5.25. Planning guidelines, most of which were revised at the last up-dating in May 1978, include operational service standards which aim to provide acceptable conditions for the majority of passengers. There are no service standards for commercial facilities. Planning guidelines provide the planner with an indication of the scale of areas he should be allowing for in his initial planning. The actual space provisions at the detailed planning stage are a matter of judgment and take into account an assessment of marketing opportunities, the anticipated traffic characteristics and any overall physical constraints which may be imposed on the terminal design. The Gatwick North Terminal development is here used to illustrate the relationship between the planning guidelines and current practice.

TABLE 5.1 **Gatwick North Terminal**

Phase 1: 5 million passengers per annum (mppa); 1,500/1,600 Busy Hour Rate (BHR).
Ultimate: 9 mppa; 2,500 BHR.

	Planned		PG estimate*	
	Phase 1 m^2	Ultimate m^2	Phase 1 m^2	Ultimate m^2
Airside				
Duty-free ⎫				
Tax-free ⎭	1,250	1,250	665	1,110
Buffet and bar	455	820	325	570
Landside				
Catering and bar	865	1,492	810	1,380
Source: BAA.				

*See note to Table 5.3.

5.26. Some comparable figures for Heathrow Terminal 3 (redevelopment) and Terminal 4 are as follows:

TABLE 5.2 **Heathrow Terminal 3 redevelopment**

12 mppa; 3000 BHR.

	Planned m^2	Adjusted* PG estimate m^2
Airside		
Duty-free ⎫		
Tax-free ⎭	1,672	890
Buffet and bar	965	710
Landside		
Catering and bar	1,940	1,890
Source: BAA.		

*See note to Table 5.3.

[1]The building is designed to accommodate 9 mppa ultimately, but under Phase I will be fitted out only for 5 mppa.

48

TABLE 5.3   **Heathrow Terminal 4**

8 mppa; 2000 BHR.

	Planned m²	Adjusted* PG estimate m²
Airside		
Duty-free ⎫ Tax-free ⎭	1,530	750
Buffet and bar	1,100	500
Landside		
Catering and bar	1,400	1,300

Source: BAA.

---

*Because planning guidelines are currently being updated, but are not yet finalised, BAA's comparisons of 'actual' versus 'Planning Guidelines' floor areas were based on the 1978 planning guidelines. BAA told us that 'there are strict limitations on the applicability of the 1978 planning guidelines to Terminals of the size of those under discussion'.

5.27. Heathrow Terminal 3's redevelopment will significantly change the space devoted to some commercial activities. For example:

TABLE 5.4   **Heathrow Terminal 3 redevelopment**

12 mppa; 3000 BHR.

	Proposed m²	Existing m²
Departures airside		
Duty- and tax-free shop (retail area)	1,672	703
Storage	592	154
	2,264	857
Arrivals		
Retail — Skyshop	104	
Car rental	190	
	294	147

Source: BAA.

5.28. The investment appraisal of such projects is discussed in paragraphs 8.10 to 8.14.

Organisation

5.29. In December 1981 the Board accepted a proposal by its Chairman that a review should be made of BAA's organisation. The existing organisation of the Authority had been developed following a study by management consultants in 1969. Priorities for the review would be:

(*a*) 'the relationship of Head Office and the airports';

(*b*) 'the current policy of maximum decentralisation';

49

(c) 'the organisation of Head Office departments'; and

(d) 'the distribution of functions within them'.

The study would be conducted by an internal team assisted by an outside consultant.

5.30. The Study Group reported in March 1982 and the Board made its decisions on the report in April 1982. The resulting changes in organisation are now known within the Authority by the name of the hotel at which discussions took place, 'Chewton Glen'. BAA told us that a general thrust of the reorganisation was to reduce the involvement of the Board in matters of detail and to continue the policy of 'maximum decentralisation to airports'. The 'Summary of Recommendations' included the following items:

(a) 'Financial delegation to the Managing Director should be increased within six months to £5 million at Heathrow and Gatwick and £2 million elsewhere, so that fewer project approvals are submitted to the Board.'

(b) 'The Board should increase its function as the major reviewer of the performance of the Authority.'

(c) 'Part-time Board members should be encouraged by the Chairman to take an informal interest in specific areas of the Authority's management based on their particular expertise.'

(d) 'The responsibility for active corporate planning should be given to the Director of Planning, including responsibility for an efficiency audit.'

(e) 'A post of Director of Marketing should be created having responsibility for planning and co-ordinating all marketing in BAA. Responsibilities should include Commercial, Property, External Relations and Market Research.'

5.31. Board decisions following the organisation study report included the following:

(a) 'The Board will consider the overall performance of the Authority as its primary function.'

(b) 'Financial delegation to the Managing Director will be increased immediately to £2 million as an interim measure, subject to a further review.'

(c) 'Part-time Board members will continue to take an informal interest in specific areas of the Authority's management based on their particular expertise and interests.'

(d) 'The Planning Director will be responsible for an expanded corporate planning function, including responsibility for efficiency auditing.'

(e) 'A Commercial Development Director will be appointed having responsibility for planning and organising all commercial development in BAA. Responsibilities will include Commercial, Property, Advertising, Publications, Promotions and Market Research.'

5.32. In May 1984 the Board conducted a three-day review of the Chewton Glen decisions and implementation. The minutes record that: 'The continued interest of part-time Board members in specific areas of the Authority's operations was welcomed by the Chairman.'

5.33. Following the Board decisions in April 1982 the post of Commercial Development Director was filled from outside BAA. The new Director took up his appointment in January 1983. In February 1984 a new Trading Department, reporting to the Commercial Development Director, was set up (see paragraph 3.26 *et seq*). In March 1985 the total number of staff employed on Trading and Property activities was:

Head Office

Full-time	Part-time	Full-time equivalent
68	7	71

Airports

Full-time	Part-time	Full-time equivalent
108	109	162

Total full-time equivalent 233

compared with a total of 125 Commercial and Property staff at Head Office and the Airports in March 1982 (see also Table 12.1).

5.34. In its present form the Trading Department has a Marketing Manager, an Information Management Manager, and a General Manager. Reporting to the last of these are six Product Managers and a Tenders and Contracts Manager. The Product Managers are responsible for, respectively, duty-free, tax-free, arrivals, duty-paid, catering and new products. Three of the present Product Managers have recently been appointed from outside BAA.

5.35. Also reporting to the Commercial Development Director are the Air Cargo Manager and the General Manager Property (both located at Head Office).

5.36. BAA's summary of the main changes in commercial functions at airports in the period 1983 to 1985 is reproduced at Appendix 5.4.

5.37. The Trading Department has specific responsibilities, including pricing, determining the range of products to be sold, and merchandising, for a wide range of activities previously known as 'commercial'. The remaining 'commercial' activities retain that name, and remain the primary responsibility of airports, although advice from the Trading Department is available. The division of activities between 'commercial' (or 'airport') and 'trading' (or 'central') is as follows:

Airport/commercial	Central/trading
Airside/aircrew transport	Duty- and tax-free shops
Transfer passenger services	Duty-paid shops
Aircraft cleaning	Car rental
Ground handling	Spectators' shops and services
Transit shed	Post offices
Fuel farms	Petrol filling stations
Taxis	Banks
Toothbrush and razor vending	Photo-machines
Bonded transit shed	Catering/food and tobacco vending
Apron loading	Flight catering
Car-parking	Advertising

51

Airport/Commercial	*Central/trading*
Spectators	Hairdresser
	Insurance
	Dry cleaning
	Hotel bookings
	Telephones
	Hotels
	Staff shops/services

BAA told us that this division was agreed at a meeting between Airport Directors and the Commercial Development Director.

5.38. A draft Internal Audit report in June 1985 on duty-paid shops concluded that adequate understanding of their respective roles by Trading Department staff and airport commercial staff had not yet been achieved. This conclusion did not appear in the final report.

5.39. The General Manager Property has responsibility for the negotiation of major leases at South-East airports, and for overall property policy and specialist advice at all airports. Otherwise property is managed by the airports. The Air Cargo Manager is available to give specialist cargo advice to the airports. Cargo is otherwise the responsibility of each airport.

5.40. The responsibility for the capital and revenue budgets for all 'commercial' activities, whether designated 'trading' or 'commercial', lies with the airports. Thus it is the airports which are responsible for achieving their trading/commercial targets. The Trading Department views this as a source of conflict with airport management, since it sees itself as having responsibility for the development of commercial income.

5.41. The Authority told us that this conflict forms part of a still unresolved issue within the organisation. The Trading Department wishes to change the current situation. It has asked initially to be given responsibility for annual expenditure of £750,000 for 'minor capital works' at airports. In future years a trading capital budget of £5 million would be sought. This would be used for the refitting and refurbishing of retail outlets. The Trading Department also wishes in the future to make 'a financial bid to each individual Airport Director' for commercial space. The agreed commercial income budgets would then be solely the responsibility of the Trading Department.

5.42. The alternative view, which could be broadly characterised as that held by airport managements, is that the total capital resources of airports are subject to many demands and opportunities in addition to those of the Trading Department. A system which would amount to allocating a portion of the total to commercial activities in advance would not only allow that department an opportunity for a more rapid response but might in doing so also give it unwarranted priority in the allocation of scarce resources which are also required for safety or operations. The ultimate decision between competing priorities ought to be left with the Airport Director.

5.43. Although the Trading Department refers to conflict between itself and the airports on financial responsibility and over the allocation of space to airport activities, BAA told us that there is no deliberate policy to produce 'creative tension'.

Conclusions

5.44. BAA encourages its part-time Board members to take an interest in specific activities according to their individual expertise and experience. There is at present no member with retailing experience, although through its commercial activities BAA now controls a major retail business. BAA's Chairman told us that he would welcome an increase in the size of the Board, to a total of perhaps 12 or 14 members, and had said so from time to time to successive Secretaries of State. This would give an increased opportunity for the recruitment of a part-time member wih retail commercial expertise. We support that view.

5.45. At the time of the 'Chewton Glen' decisions BAA declared itself in favour of a more 'pro-active' approach to corporate strategy. We take that to mean that the Board should play a more active role by laying down the framework within which important decisions should be taken, rather than only reacting to proposals coming up from the Executive. In that spirit we believe that the Board should, in approaching a decision on the provision and allocation of space in new and redeveloped terminals, tell the Executive what range of options should be considered, and require the Executive to demonstrate that the full range of commercial possibilities, within the constraints imposed by physical conditions, has been explored.

5.46. BAA told us that planning guidelines are an important means by which the Board gives general guidance on the provision of facilities at terminals. The planning guidelines relevant to our inquiry were last updated and extended in May 1978. In comparing the space which would be allocated to commercial activities in accordance with those guidelines with that actually planned for Heathrow Terminal 4 and Terminal 3 (redeveloped) and Gatwick North Terminal (9 mppa), BAA emphasised the limitations of the guidelines for such large terminals. We believe that planning guidelines, which are currently being updated, should be updated more frequently; and that care should be taken to ensure they are appropriate to facilities on the scale likely to be planned.

5.47. The setting of targets at several levels of the organisation, in addition to budget forecasts, is a quite recent innovation in BAA. The Authority's Board has decided that targets should be set so as to present greater challenges to management than are presented by budget forecasts. BAA's Chairman believes that commercial performance in the past has not been satisfactory in relation to potential, and there has not yet been time for the new Trading Department to have a significant impact. It seems, therefore, that BAA's current targets should be set at a level significantly higher than past trends would indicate. The Board will be able to set feasible but more challenging targets for commercial performance for the year ensuing if it can achieve greater understanding of the relative roles of, on the one hand, managerial effectiveness and other factors largely under BAA's control and, on the other hand, those external factors which are largely outside its control. (See our proposal in paragraph 4.33.)

5.48. In general, the organisational changes resulting from 'Chewton Glen' reinforced BAA's trend towards decentralisation, with the exception of the new arrangements made for the organisation of commercial functions, which went against this trend. The Commercial Development Director took up his post at the end of January 1983. The central Trading Department was established in February 1984. BAA says it is too early to be sure that the new commercial organisation fulfils Chewton Glen's hopes for it. Accepting that, the Chewton Glen decision on commercial matters seems to us to have been soundly based.

5.49. The Commercial Development Director is responsible for advising BAA on the exploitation of all commercial potential at its airports. In setting up the Trading Department he has given priority to the retailing activities at terminals. In due course it will be necessary to ensure that the potential of other commercial activities including, for example, car parks, cargo and property receives the attention already given to retailing.

5.50. The division of responsibility between the Trading Department and the airport managements for achieving trading results at airports, and for revenue and capital budgets, as established since Chewton Glen, is currently being debated within BAA. We consider that the present arrangements are satisfactory. The Commercial Development Director should retain his responsibility for advising BAA on the exploitation of all commercial potential and the Director or General Manager of an airport should have final responsibility for all activities at his airport.

CHAPTER 6

Information and computing

Management information

6.1. In the previous chapter we reviewed BAA's strategy, the role of its main Board and the Authority's formal planning. The main information received routinely by the Board is in BAA's Monthly Management Report which is circulated also to senior management (General Managers and above). The commercial analysis and the performance indicator annex are produced on a quarterly basis.

6.2. The Monthly Management Report for December 1984 was tabled at the meeting of the Board in February 1985. A section on commercial activity followed those on Traffic and Finance; this last contained details of income including that from Trading concessions and from rents and services. The commercial section consisted of a ten-page commentary under these sub-headings:

promotional activities

duty- and tax-free

duty-paid

catering

other concessions

new products

air cargo

There was no reference to income from property.

6.3. A later section entitled 'Services to Passengers' had as its main sub-sections:

complaints analysis (related mainly to BAA areas of responsibility)

baggage reclaim analysis

passenger delays.

6.4. An annex to the Monthly Management Report for December 1984 contained performance indicators. The indicators most relevant to commercial activities were:

duty- and tax-free income per international departing passenger (IDP);

other concession income per passenger;

gross property income; and

complaints per 100,000 passengers.

Examples of the results of complaints analysis, and of commercial performance indicators, are given in paragraphs 13.29 and 13.30.

6.5. The Management Accounting Reporting System (MARS) reports are produced monthly and are given 'wide circulation' within the Authority. They are discussed in paragraph 7.21 *et seq.*

6.6. A Commercial Revenue Analysis report is produced monthly on a bureau computer and 'circulated widely' within the Trading Department. (Relevant sections of the report are also sent to airport managements.) It gives BAA revenue for the previous month, the percentage growth in revenue over the same month in the previous year, and the percentage growth in income per passenger (per IDP for duty- and tax-free) over the same month in the previous year. The report also includes an end-of-year forecast of revenue and compares this with the figures from the last budget review.

Computing

6.7. Before looking at particular aspects of BAA's use of computers it is worth noting its approach to computing before 1983, when an outside consultancy was commissioned to review the Authority's information processing strategy. The Authority told us that it had encouraged as many of its staff as possible to take an interest in computing. BAA told us:

We let people go off and do what they thought was right and gave them help where we could.

[The Managing Director] judged it and still judge[s] it to have been a very important and beneficial period in the BAA that the knowledge of and the use of computers in many, many areas was encouraged and not dampened by some simplistic approach from the centre ...

Computerised property management system

6.8. BAA's first computerised property management system was installed at Heathrow in July 1976. A feasibility report in April 1981 proposed a new system for Gatwick and Stansted, which Heathrow was expected eventually to adopt. The system became operational on the following dates: Gatwick, January 1984; Heathrow, April 1984; Stansted, November 1984. At an early stage of our inquiry BAA expressed ' serious ... concern ' over the new system and told us that a review was being carried out. We asked for a statement on the system which would be as up-to-date as possible within the timetable for our inquiry. BAA's statement of 28 June 1985 is reproduced at Appendix 6.1.

6.9. In addition to its intrinsic relevance to our inquiry, we were interested in whether the computerised property management system's problems were indicative of problems in computing experienced more generally by BAA. The 1983 report (see paragraph 6.7) reviewed the Authority's computing achievements and problems to date and suggested major changes.

Review of information processing strategy 1983

6.10. The consultancy reported on its review in May 1983. BAA had asked it:

(i) To identify BAA's actual and potential information processing requirements through discussion with the main users.

56

(ii) To review the resources currently available within the Management Services function, and assess the extent to which these appeared to meet BAA's actual and potential requirements.

(iii) In the light of the assessment, to review the range of options available, and recommend a strategic plan for future information processing activities. The plan should particularly consider the balance and co-ordination between various types of hardware.

(iv) To assess the strengths and weaknesses of the present organisation structure, to analyse the skills currently available and to recommend a future management structure for information processing activities. The structure should be sufficiently flexible to allow advantage to be taken of evolving technology.

6.11. In the Introduction to the Management Summary of its report the consultancy acknowledged that BAA's approach to information processing showed the Authority's desire to exploit developments in information technology to the full. Micro-computing and specialist information systems were especially praiseworthy. However, there had been inadequate co-ordination. Moreover, while Head Office functions were adequately supported by Management Services' facilities, airport management in its day-to-day operations was not properly catered for. Organisational changes were needed to improve co-ordination. BAA would have to make major changes in its approach to information processing.

6.12. In a paper presented to the Authority's Executive in September 1983 the Personnel Director reported:

(a) The areas of concern can be summarised as

—the present largely unco-ordinated approach to systems development which tends to offer sub-optimal solutions, both for airport and corporate requirements;

—the difficulty experienced by users in gaining access to, and making effective use of, information held in the central computer for existing systems;

—the lengthy time taken to develop new systems;

—the comparative lack of systems addressing management information needs;

—the inadequacy of resources to support the development of airport systems;

—the lack of a single point of contact in Management Services for managers to approach to consider the best type of application for their needs;

—the lack of a mechanism for Directors to become involved in defining information processing policy.

(b) The consultants concluded that there is considerable scope for information processing to 'assist BAA to be as profitable as possible in all areas'.

(c) To achieve this the consultants had put forward a strategy with three main themes:

—consistency of data across BAA;

—a 'systems architecture' which offered both speedy development of major systems, and ease of use and access by end users;

—a co-ordinated approach with Management Services responsible for all policy on administrative information processing.

6.13. During the Executive's discussion of the report the Heathrow Airport Director suggested that his airport should set up its own data processing function with a Heathrow-based team responsible for software. The Personnel Director said that Management Services would contain a 'Management Group' dealing solely with airport systems requirements. The Managing Director agreed that some such staff could be based at Heathrow provided they were under Management Services' control. It was further agreed that departments would budget for some of their own computer needs. Beyond that the main recommendations noted in paragraph 6.12(c) were accepted.

6.14. Given BAA's acceptance of the main 1983 recommendations, particularly those concerning improved co-ordination of computing throughout BAA, we were interested in the present state of computing, which falls within the Authority's Management Services Department.

Management Services

6.15. Management Services has three major functions:

(a) developing strategies and plans to match the corporate information processing policy;

(b) developing systems to satisfy the business needs of the Authority; and

(c) providing and operating the technical elements necessary to run and support the systems.

6.16. At our request, the Head of Management Services prepared a paper which described both the organisation and activities of the department in general, and those activities which are especially relevant to BAA's commercial functions. The paper's main headings were:

(a) Organisation and equipment;

(b) Commercial systems—current;

(c) Further plans for commercial systems;

(d) Methods and standards; and

(e) Further plans for Management Services.

The summary in paragraphs 6.17 to 6.21 is based largely on this paper, supplemented by interviews conducted by our staff.

6.17. The Personnel Director is responsible at Executive level for Management Services. He reports formally to the Executive every six months. He chairs the Information Processing Sub-Committee of the Executive, which met for the first time in June 1985. Another committee is the Computer Projects Working Group, which includes representatives of each airport and Head Office department, advises the Head of Management Services on priorities amongst projects, and acts as a forum for discussion.

6.18. The Head of Management Services, who reports to the Personnel Director at Head Office, was appointed in December 1984. The post, which is a new one and was filled from outside BAA, is at Deputy Director level. She is responsible for:

(a) setting and implementing the corporate policy on information processing; developing comprehensive plans for information processing;

(b) setting and monitoring standards on data, hardware, software and methodologies;

(c) co-ordinating the work of information processing groups at airports and in other departments;

(d) developing and implementing corporate solutions;

(e) approving information processing developments carried out by groups outside Management Services; and

(f) budgeting for, installing and operating corporate data networks, and computer facilities.

6.19. The Head of Management Services is supported by:

(a) the General Manager, Management Services;

(b) the Business Systems Manager, who is responsible for identifying users' needs and developing appropriate systems; and

(c) the Computing Services Manager, responsible for hardware, software, data management, data communications and technology training.

6.20. The current systems serving primarily the commercial functions of BAA are:

(a) concessions accounting/commercial performance;

(b) duty-free point-of-sale analysis;

(c) the bureau-run system (see paragraph 6.6);

(d) property management system (see paragraph 6.8).

Other relevant systems include:

(e) general ledger (see paragraph 7.25 et seq);

(f) PRESTEL;

(g) current office automation; and

(h) some systems with more general application.

The interaction between present systems is shown in the diagram in Appendix 6.2.

6.21. In addition to the Trading Department's planned information system (see paragraph 6.24 *et seq*), possible changes or developments in the computerised property management system, and the recently introduced general ledger system, future plans for commercial systems include enhanced Electronic Point-of-Sale (EPOS) data capture at concessionaires' outlets at BAA airports and the development of an 'automated office'.

6.22. At present Management Services does not charge other BAA departments for the use of its services (people, software and computer time). From April 1985 all Management Services activities were costed against projects and user departments. BAA intends to formulate charging rates for both staff and central computers so that actual charging can begin by April 1986.

6.23. Since 1983 there has been an increasing tendency for airports to set up units to handle information processing. At Heathrow the Planning and Traffic section contains a Management Information systems team. Scottish Airports Head Office has a liaison officer for information processing. In addition, Head Office Trading Department has a Information Management Manager.

Trading Department computer system

6.24. The Trading Department's planned information system is of particular relevance to our inquiry. While recognising that it is still at a rather early stage of development, we looked at it in some detail.

6.25. Shortly after it was established the Trading Department, together with Management Services, commissioned an outside consultancy (different from that which prepared the 1983 report) to review the computer system requirements for the Trading Department. The consultants' report was presented in May 1984. The review led to a feasibility study whose objective was to expand the role of the earlier study to include:

(*a*) identifying user requirements in more detail, including those of airports;

(*b*) examining existing Trading Department information systems in more detail;

(*c*) reviewing and evaluating alternative approaches to meeting the requirements identified; and

(*d*) preparing a Feasibility Report according to PROMPT II¹standards which sets out the business case for development and includes an implementation plan and cost estimate.

6.26. The report's ' Management Summary ' concluded that the development of a computer system for the Trading Department would bring major benefits to BAA. Total staff costs of implementing the new system would be about £175,000. Software costs would add at least a further £30,000. Operating costs might be of the order of £25,000 per annum. Against these costs, savings in payments to third parties for data processing would be some £240,000 per annum (from which could be subtracted at most £40,000 per annum for BAA hardware and machine time costs). Other benefits would include the facility for Trading and Airport staff to:

(*a*) monitor commercial performance and thereby identify opportunities for significantly increasing BAA revenue;

(*b*) evaluate the effect of promotions and other marketing actions and react accordingly;

¹PROMPT is an acronym for *P*roject, *R*esource, *O*rganisation, *M*anagement, and *P*lanning *T*echniques, developed by Simpact Systems Limited.

(c) gain more understanding of the factors affecting commercial performance in order to exert better control over Trading activities; and

(d) forecast commercial performance.

6.27. According to the report, information then available to the Trading Department and to commercial staff at airports was not consistent, was not sufficiently accurate and was not produced quickly enough. Problems included:

(a) Data inputs and initial processing were not controlled adequately. Inaccurate and out-of-date information resulted.

(b) Systems were not integrated.

(c) Systems were difficult to modify.

6.28. Timely, accurate and consistent information was required for the following main categories:

(a) concessionaires' monthly sales and BAA's income by appropriate product group;

(b) passenger statistics;

(c) detailed point-of-sale information;

(d) information from market research surveys; and

(e) information on concessions including floor areas and product percentage margins, and BAA spending on concessions.

Access to information should be available via regular reports and *ad hoc* queries. Information should be capable of graphical presentation.

6.29. BAA decided in November 1984 to implement this proposed system. The 'user specification' stage was completed by the end of March 1985. The systems design stage was completed on schedule at the end of July 1985. The original development costs were estimated to be £205,000; the latest estimate (June 1985) for the total development cost was just under £400,000. BAA told us that the increase was due to the inclusion of the hardware and training costs as a direct cost to the project rather than a corporate cost outside the project. The annual running costs were estimated at a total of £88,000. The estimate of 'annual tangible benefits' (savings) remained at £240,000.

Conclusions and recommendations

6.30. BAA has in recent years noted deficiencies in the management information relevant to its commercial activities and has developed, or begun to develop, new systems to remedy these deficiencies.

6.31. Continuing difficulties with the property system suggest that not all the problems identified in the 1983 review of the whole of the Authority's information processing strategy have been solved.

6.32. At an early stage in our inquiry the Authority admitted to 'serious . . . concern' over its new computerised property management system. BAA's statement of 28 June 1985 on this system is reproduced at Appendix 6.1. Past mistakes are evident, and most important and urgent decisions, particularly concerning Heathrow, remain to be taken. BAA is now seeking information about computerised property management systems recently developed elsewhere.

6.33. In view of our proposal in paragraph 5.50 that final responsibility for all activities at an airport, including Trading and other commercial activities, should remain with its Director or General Manager it will be necessary to ensure that the new computerised Trading Information System meets the specific requirements of the airport management responsible for Trading performance.

CHAPTER 7

Financial framework

7.1. BAA has defined its primary objective as being to respond to the present and future needs of air transport in an efficient and profitable way by operating, planning and developing its airports so that air travellers and cargo may pass through safely, swiftly and as conveniently as possible. In support of this objective the Authority's principal financial policy is to ensure as far as possible that it meets the financial and performance aims, external financing limits and other targets agreed with the Government from time to time.

7.2. The Authority's statutory financial duties are outlined in sections 3 to 8 and 21 of the Airports Authority Act 1975, the main provisions of which are summarised below:

(a) to break even on revenue account taking one year with another;

(b) in framing and carrying out proposals involving substantial outlay on capital account, to act on lines settled from time to time with the approval of the Secretary of State;

(c) to apply revenue surpluses in such manner as the Secretary of State, with the approval of the Treasury, and after consultation with the Chairman of the Authority, may direct; and

(d) to report on its performance to the Secretary of State as soon as possible after the end of each accounting year, including such information on its plans, past and present activities and financial position as the Secretary of State may direct, and attaching a copy of its statement of accounts and any report on the accounts made by the auditors.

7.3. Table 7.1 shows the Authority's income and current cost profits for each of the last five years and indicates that commercial activities have subsidised traffic operations in each of those years.

7.4. The Act also prescribes limits on the amounts that the Authority may borrow. Temporary loans are not to exceed such limit as the Secretary of State may impose by direction with the approval of the Treasury (at present £50 million). Other borrowings may be made for capital expenditure, the provision of working capital and analogous purposes. The aggregate of all such borrowings and the amount outstanding on the Authority's commencing capital debt[1] is not to exceed £200 million. At 31 March 1985 BAA's total outstanding debt amounted to £91·6 million.

7.5. Each year the Government also sets an external financing limit (EFL) which limits the extent to which BAA can borrow money. The Authority has operated within these limits in recent years as is shown in Table 7.2.

---

[1] The debt which under the provisions of the Airports Authority Act 1965 was assumed by the Authority as a debt due to the then Minister of Aviation. At the time of the 1975 Act this debt had been reduced to £52·91 million and at 31 March 1985 it stood at £38·8 million.

TABLE 7.1 **BAA: income and current cost trading profits**

£ million

	1980–81	1981–82	1982—83	1983–84	1984–85
Traffic operations					
Income	152·3	160·4	152·5	166·9	182·6
Expenditure	156·3	169·7	177·0	193·0	204·3
(Loss)	(4·0)	(9·3)	(24·5)	(26·1)	(21·7)
Commercial operations					
Income	101·7	117·1	131·2	149·3	179·0
Expenditure	59·8	68·1	68·1	71·6	82·7
Profit	41·9	49·0	63·1	77·7	96·3
Current cost trading profit	37·9	39·7	38·6	51·6	74·6

Source: BAA.

Note: The profits shown above for 1982–83 and 1984–85 are before charging additional depreciation of £3·6 million and £2·6 million respectively arising from asset life revisions. See note to Table 4.1.

TABLE 7.2 **EFL**

£ million

	Limit	Actual
1980–81	19·0	18·3
1981–82	14·0	1·9
1982–83	48·0	1·7
1983–84	32·7	17·9
1984–85	10·0	9·6

Source: BAA.

7.6. BAA told us that the management of its funds was highly centralised. Most receipts were received and processed centrally (although, exceptionally, Scottish concessionaires paid Scottish airports direct) and airports held funds only to the extent necessary for such minor items as cash wages (applicable to only about 1 per cent of employees), staff expenses, claims etc. Cash control did not generally give rise to problems as most receipts were from trade debtors (for example, aircraft landing charges) and concessionaires rather than from the general public.

7.7. The Authority also agrees financial targets and performance aims with the Secretary of State after consultation with the airlines and trade unions. For the years 1980–81 to 1982–83 inclusive these were as follows:

(a) *Return on net assets.* To achieve on average a rate of return of 6 per cent per annum on net assets revalued at current cost, coupled with the supplementary target of moving towards CCA break even at the four Scottish airports.

(b) *Costs per passenger.* To reduce costs per passenger on average by 2·5 per cent per annum—at constant prices and excluding depreciation and net payments to the security fund (7·3 per cent over the three-year period).

(c) *Productivity.* To increase the number of passengers handled per employee (excluding security and trainees) by an average 3 per cent per annum (9·3 per cent over the three-year period).

7.8. Table 7.3 shows the Authority did not achieve these targets. BAA told us that when it agreed them with the Government, both parties were expecting traffic growth broadly in line with the levels of previous years. In the event there were only a minimal increase in passenger numbers during the period and this had a marked effect on BAA's ability to improve its performance to the extent required by the targets.

TABLE 7.3   **Government targets, 1980–81 to 1982–83**

	Target	per cent Achievement
Return on net assets	6·0	5·0
Costs per passenger (percentage reduction)	7·3	1·1
Passengers per employee (percentage increase)	9·3	7·0

Source: BAA.

7.9. For the years 1983–84 to 1985–86 the targets were changed to the following:

(a) *Return on net assets.* To achieve on average a minimum annual rate of return on average net assets of 3 per cent plus one-fifth of the annual percentage growth in terminal passengers on a cumulative basis in each successive year, coupled with the supplementary objective of achieving break even at the Scottish airports within the three-year period.

(b) *Costs per passenger.* To reduce costs (at constant prices and excluding depreciation) per terminal passenger by 0·5 per cent per annum, plus an additional reduction equivalent to two-fifths of the percentage growth in terminal passengers over the three-year period.

(c) *Productivity.* To increase the number of terminal passengers per payroll hour by 0·5 per cent per annum plus two-fifths of the percentage growth in terminal passengers over the three-year period.

7.10. Each target now combines a basic underpinning element with a variable growth-related factor and reflects both:

(a) the dependence of the Authority's income on changes in the economic climate and airline performance, over which it has no control; and

(b) the nature of its costs, which are either largely related to the provision of capacity and fixed in nature, or are outside the control of the Authority (eg rates and police costs).

7.11. The targets agreed within the Authority between the Board and the Managing Director, between the Managing Director and those reporting to him, and between directors and their line managers and at lower levels (see paragraph 5.13 *et seq*) are expected to be consistent with the achievement of the targets agreed between the Authority and the Secretary of State. For example, the Government target to reduce costs per terminal passenger by 0·5 per cent per annum plus an additional reduction equivalent to two-fifths of the percentage growth in terminal passengers over the three-year period 1983–84 to 1985–86 is reflected in the 1985–86 target agreed between the Board and the Managing Director for the reduction of costs per passenger by 3 per cent. This in turn is reflected in the targets agreed between the Managing Director and directors to contain within 1 per cent the rise in costs per passenger at Heathrow, resulting from the opening of Terminal 4, and to reduce costs per passenger at Gatwick by 4·5 per cent, and at the Scottish airports by 3 per cent.

7.12. The Authority provided us with the figures in Table 7.4 which show that it expects to meet these new targets for the current three-year period.

TABLE 7.4 **Government targets, 1983–84 to 1985–86**

		per cent
	Target	Projected achievement
Return on net assets	5·9	6·4
Costs per passenger (percentage reduction)	10·5	11·7
Passengers per payroll hour (percentage increase)	10·0	14·6

Source: BAA.

Budget-setting

7.13. The Authority's corporate planning procedures are described in detail in Appendix 5.3. In this chapter we refer to them only to the extent necessary to describe the Authority's budgetary control methods.

7.14. At the start of the corporate planning cycle in May/June the Board agrees three major planning inputs: the objectives, the targets and the traffic forecasts. It then sets specific numeric income, cost and profit targets for the immediate future and highlights areas of the business requiring additional development within the five-year period of the Corporate Plan. Senior directors and managers meet in July and agree the overall framework, assumptions and timetables for the preparation of business plans. At this stage agreement is reached on the input of commercial development into the planning process.

7.15. The seven airports constitute discrete business units operating within the framework of group policy and each airport is required to prepare its own business plan each year on the basis of the corporate assumptions and guidelines. Plans are prepared over a four-month period and submitted in late autumn. Each plan is reviewed by the Managing Director and any changes made are finalised by January. The preparation of the budget and four-year financial forecasts is integrated with the writing of the business plans. The budgets show the financial implications of implementing the plans. The Corporate Plan is finally approved in March each year.

7.16. Year one is broken down to cost centres and is an instrument of financial control, but years two to five are global forecasts broken down only to main profit centres, namely airports and Head Office director functions.

7.17. The accounting period is based on the calendar month. Considerable attention is paid to phasing the budget for seasonal factors such as variations in traffic levels.

7.18. All BAA's budgetary control and management accounting is carried out in CCA terms and the management accounts are integrated with the financial accounts down to the trading profit level, using the same computerised base.

7.19. Budgets for certain items, such as insurance and irrecoverable VAT, are held centrally and not allocated to cost centres, although actual expenditure incurred is indirectly charged to airport profit and loss accounts. The Authority intends that expenditure will only be attributed to cost centres if the budget-holder is in a position to exercise direct control over such expenditure.

7.20. The Authority prepares its budgets for the purposes of income and cost control and for planning its business for the year ahead. The minimum objective is to operate within budget, and the targets which are set are more stretching. Thus the budgeting system serves a different purpose from the targeting system. Generally speaking, budgets are prepared from the bottom up, but are then 'squeezed' from the top, which leads to pressure on the lower levels of the budget hierarchy. Although BAA does not formally use zero-based budgeting techniques, it told us that its annual planning process involved an objective assessment of the resources necessary to provide the required levels of service and that it recalculated expenditure each year rather than merely making incremental adjustments to previous years' figures. Budgets, once approved, are not revised during the year although estimates of the out-turn for the year are updated each quarter.

Monitoring performance against budget

7.21. The management accounting system in use is known as MARS (Management Accounting Reporting System) but this is in the process of being superseded. It is a centralised, computerised system. Performance is monitored, reviewed and reported to the Board and to line management on a monthly basis. The out-turn statements (that is, the comparisons of actual performance with budget) are classified by expense headings, but not by activities. They are normally produced by MARS on the tenth day of the following month, and distributed to all cost centre managers. Airport managements receive copies of the out-turn statements for all cost centres at their airports and the airport Finance Managers brief their airport directors on the results shown. Airports are substantially self-contained management units and airport directors, advised by their airport Financial Managers, are primarily responsible for monitoring the performance of their subordinate managers.

7.22. The four Scottish airports operate on similar principles: inputs are fed in by the airports to MARS, but the output statements go to the Scottish director, at Scottish Head Office, as well as to the four airport managers.

7.23. The Budget Committee, which is chaired by the Managing Director, meets four times a year to consider the out-turn statements for the total business, the seven airports individually and each Head Office director function.

Significant variances are taken up with the airport or Head Office director concerned, and by him with his subordinate managers.

7.24. Appendix 7.1 compares the Authority's budgets with out-turns for each of the last five years.

The new 'general ledger' system

7.25. A new computerised management and financial accounting and information system known as 'general ledger' was introduced from 1 April 1985 with a view to superseding MARS. This new system will capture more detailed data at a lower level and will be able to handle many more finance codes and cost centres than MARS. Improved allocations of expenditure should then enable a more accurate basis to be established for measuring the results of activities, pricing and internal charging. The aim is to provide all levels of management with timely, accurate and relevant financial and other management information as a basis for sound decision-making.

7.26. Further modifications to the existing BAA feeder systems[1] are planned so as to derive the full benefit of the new system. These are unlikely to be completed before 1986.

7.27. In 1984–85 BAA's income from commercial activities amounted to £179·0 million and expenditure recorded as incurred on such activities to £82·7 million, giving a reported profit on them of £96·3 million (see Table 7.1). Approximately 33 per cent of the expenditure was direct expenditure, 43 per cent was indirect expenditure and 24 per cent was common overheads, administration and Head Office expenses.

7.28. BAA told us that the general ledger system would enable expenditure to be more accurately attributed to activities. In the case of direct expenditure, far greater cost centre detail would be available, which would enable a more accurate system for the attribution of costs to be established, including the development of a system for attributing notional rents based on open market property values. It would offer improved facilities for the allocation of indirect expenditure, common overheads, administration and Head Office expenses. As a result, a substantial improvement in the attribution of costs to commercial activities would be possible.

7.29. Expenditure on such items as the upkeep of terminal concourses and airport administration is normally allocated wholly to traffic operations.

Board Audit Committee

7.30. The Board Audit Committee was first established in 1977. It was reconstituted in November 1983 to comprise four non-executive Board members, one of whom was chairman, and the Director of Planning.[2] It was then given new terms of reference. Its role and function now is to review and monitor the

---

[1] A feeder system will collect input data and process them by computer program (known as automated interface) to the general ledger.

[2] On 1 April 1985 the Managing Director replaced the Director of Planning as a member of the Audit Committee.

arrangements for securing economy, efficiency and effectiveness in the use of resources within the Authority and to report its findings annually to the Board.

7.31. The responsibility of the main Board to ensure the sufficiency of its accounts and finances was then delegated to the Audit Committee. The external auditors thus now make representations to the Audit Committee on the annual financial report and internal financing controls and can be questioned by its members. The Committee also makes recommendations on the appointment and remuneration of the external auditors and reviews their findings.

7.32. The Finance Director and the Chief Internal Auditor (CIA) are required to attend all meetings of the Audit Committee and to prepare papers for it as necessary. The external auditors attend when requested.

External audit

7.33. The external auditors attend annually at a meeting of the Audit Committee to present the draft annual accounts, report their interim audit findings and give an oral report on the final audit; and to explain the scope of the audit for the past year and how their findings might affect the next year's audit.

7.34. Although the external auditors do not attend other meetings of the Audit Committee unless so required, they make written submissions on important matters as necessary.

7.35. Following the completion of the audit each year they send the Finance Director a letter setting out any areas of weakness uncovered during the audit. The Finance Director responds to the letter explaining the reasons for the weaknesses and detailing the action he intends taking to rectify them. This letter, together with the response, is submitted to the Audit Committee.

7.36. The Audit Committee will call upon the external auditors for additional assistance if this is necessary to supplement the internal auditors' resources, particularly where specialist knowledge is required.

Internal audit

7.37. Internal audit is a Head Office function headed by the CIA. Until 1982 the CIA reported to the Finance Director and his work was concerned primarily with financial auditing and the auditing of concessionaires' returns. In that year, following the major organisation study referred to in paragraph 5.29 *et seq*, it was decided to introduce the concept of efficiency audit by including efficiency and value for money in the work of the Internal Audit branch, and by transferring the responsibility for it to the Planning Director who until 31 March 1985 was a member of the Audit Committee and of the Board.[1] We were told that the reason for the transfer was because of the wider role of the Planning Director in corporate planning and performance measurement and because the Planning function is probably the most remote of all Head Office functions from operational management.

---

[1] The Managing Director told us ' I do not think it has been formally decided yet whether the internal audit department will always report to a full-time Board member. It would seem to me to be a reasonable thing to aim for.'

7.38. The CIA has a team of nine auditors with the following backgrounds:

Accountancy	4
System analysis (Computer audit)	1
Organisation and methods	1
Engineering	1
Airport management	2
	9

7.39. The CIA is graded below the grade of Airport General Manager and the members of his branch are graded at or below the grades of the Finance Managers at airports with whom they have frequent dealings.

7.40. The work of internal audit now includes financial regularity auditing, efficiency audit and the audit of concessions and concessionaires' systems. It also includes the provision of systems advice and the investigation of suspected fraud.

7.41. At the start of each financial year the CIA prepares an audit programme. Considerations taken into account are the importance and vulnerability of the area proposed for audit and the lapse of time since it was last audited. The programme is agreed with the Planning Director who then submits it to the Managing Director for final approval. The Audit Committee is informed of the final programme (as is the Executive Committee of the Authority) but its approval is not sought.

7.42. In the three years 1982–83 to 1984–85 13 concession audits were undertaken, covering 47 out of 170 concessions at the Authority's seven airports. BAA told us that the value of the 47 concessions audited represented £84 million out of a total concession income for 1983–84 of £98·8 million.

7.43. The audit cycle begins with the director or directors of the airport or Head Office function concerned being informed that an audit is to be carried out. A preliminary review of the subject is then undertaken to determine the extent and scope of the work required before terms of reference are submitted to the director concerned for comment and agreement. Once he has agreed them the audit may proceed.

7.44. Managers are informed of any findings calling for immediate remedial action. On the completion of the audit a draft report is produced, setting out findings, conclusions and recommendations. Space is also left in the draft for the manager's contribution to the action paragraphs.

7.45. The final report, including the proposed action to be taken, is issued to the director or directors concerned and copied to the Planning Director and the Managing Director. The Audit Committee receives progress reports on audit findings and managers' responses, but does not normally receive copies of individual internal audit reports, although its members have access to them on request.

7.46. BAA supplied us with copies of some audit reports relating to concession operations. These were well prepared and the procedures for presentation, response, review and submission to higher levels of management were adequate, but the time taken to provide responses was tending to lengthen. BAA attributed this to the fact that the Trading Department was a new department, to its involvement in this inquiry and to the greater complexity of audit reports now that efficiency aspects are covered.

7.47. The CIA meets several times a year with the external auditors to discuss his audit programme, the relationship between external and internal audit work, suggestions on items for future programmes, auditors' 'management' letters and work carried out by the internal audit branch during the year.

Monitoring and profitability of concessionaires

7.48. Most concession agreements give BAA the right of access to the concessionaire's books and accounts including, in the case of duty- and tax-free shops, cost and management accounts. BAA told us that this clause is included to assist in the detection of possible fraud, and that it does not concern itself with the level of profits earned by concessionaires, nor does it attempt to carry out an audit of this aspect. It rarely if ever exercised this right of access and if it were to do so other than in exceptional circumstances concessionaires might resent it as an intrusion. It usually only verifies the receipt of payments due to it under the agreements and checks that conditions as to prices charged and quality of service are complied with.

Financial results of commercial activities

7.49. BAA provided us with certain detailed analyses of the financial results of its commercial activities. It told us that these should not in all cases be taken as the definitive financial results of those activities as certain costs could only be allocated on an arbitrary basis. These analyses are set out in Table 7.5 and Appendices 7.2, 7.3 and 7.4.

7.50. A statement of CCA income and expenditure by airport is included each year in the Authority's Annual Report and Accounts. This analyses income, expenditure and profit between traffic and commercial activities at each airport. These figures also enter into the key financial figures published elsewhere in the Annual Reports.

7.51. BAA told us that the separation of traffic from commercial costs and revenues in its Annual Reports had a historical background, derived from the time when the airports were operated by the Government, and that the continued publication of these figures was by Ministerial direction. A few years ago it had made representations to the Secretary of State that these figures should no longer be published, but this request had not been acceded to.

Conclusions

7.52. During the period 1980–81 to 1982–83 BAA did not achieve the targets set by Government for returns on net assets and for reductions in costs per

	1980–81 £m	1981–82 £m	1982–83 £m	1983–84 £m	1984–85 £m	Increase 1980–81 to 1984–85 %
Duty-free liquor	16·7	17·5	19·6	22·0	25·6	53
Duty-free tobacco products	11·4	12·3	13·7	15·3	18·1	59
Other tax-free	9·7	12·0	14·7	19·3	25·4	162
Tax- and duty-paid	6·0	6·4	7·4	8·5	10·1	68
Catering	4·1	4·7	4·6	5·3	6·3	54
Advertising	0·5	0·7	0·8	1·3	1·9	280
Car hire	2·5	3·3	3·7	4·2	5·2	108
Parking	9·3	10·7	12·4	13·9	16·3	75
Other concession income	5·1	6·8	7·4	9·0	11·0	116
Advertising administered by concessionaires	—	—	—	—	(1·0)	N/A
Total concession income	65·3	74·4	84·3	98·8	118·9	82
Rents and services	36·1	42·4	46·6	49·9	59·3	64
Miscellaneous	0·3	0·3	0·3	0·6	0·8	N/A
Total commercial income	101·7	117·1	131·2	149·3	179·0	76

Source: BAA.

Note: The item ' Advertising administered by concessionaires ' represents that expenditure incurred on commercial advertising which has been deducted from concessionaires' payments to BAA.

passenger and passengers per employee. This was mainly due, the Authority told us, to there being less traffic growth during the period than had been expected when the targets were set. The targets for the period 1983–84 to 1985–86 have been modified and overall BAA expects to achieve them.

7.53. During recent years the Authority has exceeded its concession income budgets and has kept within its expenditure budgets. This may suggest that budgets should be made more rigorous and challenging and we recommend that BAA reviews its budget-setting procedures with these considerations in mind.

7.54. The Authority's Annual Reports show that its profits on commercial activities subsidise its traffic operations. However, a substantial proportion of its expenditure is not directly attributable to particular activities. There is thus an element of judgment in the allocation of this expenditure between traffic operations and commercial activities, which may affect the extent to which its reported results for each activity are meaningful.

7.55. BAA told us that this would not affect its traffic charges, which are determined on the basis of long run marginal costs and set at the level necessary to achieve the Authority's target return on capital after allowing for its income from commercial activities.

7.56. We nevertheless attach importance to the results of the Authority's activities at different airports being reported as clearly as possible, both for management accounting purposes and in its Annual Reports. They indicate the extent to which commercial activities support traffic operations; they may affect decisions on facilities to be provided for particular activities; and they are relevant in considering the trade-off between profit maximisation from commercial activities and the ease and efficiency of passenger and cargo movements.

7.57. We believe that the procedures used by BAA in allocating expenditure between its various activities are capable of refinement and improvement. The Authority has recognised this and is seeking to improve the accuracy of its accounts by the introduction of its new ' general ledger ' management accounting and information system. We hope that it will take advantage of the facilities offered by the new system to attribute as much expenditure as possible to particular activities and airports. One way in which this can be done is by establishing subsidiary cost centres from which usage can be charged out on a measured basis. This is particularly relevant in the case of land and buildings held by the Authority either freehold or under long leases; the new system would facilitate the attribution of notional rents based on open market values.

7.58. We have also considered what is the best treatment of expenditure, firstly on the upkeep of those areas in an airport, such as general passenger concourses and roads, which are used both for the movement of passengers and to give access to commercial services, and secondly on airport administration. It has been suggested that BAA's present practice, which is normally to allocate such expenditure wholly to traffic operations, introduces a bias in favour of commercial activities and thus exaggerates the extent to which commercial activities support traffic operations. Such a view implies that commercial activities are of comparable significance to the Authority's primary objective to operate, plan and develop its airports so that air travellers and cargo may pass through safely, swiftly and as conveniently as possible.

7.59. The Authority told us that in practice it had to provide commercial services as well as facilities for the movement of passengers. The distinction in its Accounts between traffic operations and commercial activities was therefore not meaningful and it continued to present them in that form only because the Secretary of State required it to do so. We take the view that a distinction can and should be drawn between the services provided by the Authority in connection with its traffic operations and those provided in connection with its commercial activities, even if in practice it is necessary for it to provide both types of service, and that its published Report and Accounts should therefore continue to show separately the results of each service at each airport. We also regard the commercial services and facilities provided by the Authority as ancillary to its traffic operations and in these particular circumstances we believe it to be correct in attributing to traffic operations all expenditure that is not clearly identifiable with the provision of commercial facilities and services.

7.60. We therefore recommend that the Authority should maintain its present practice of showing separately in its Annual Report and Accounts the results of its traffic operations and its commercial activities at each of its airports, and that it should continue to do so if privatisation takes place. After privatisation, it would continue to enjoy a substantial degree of monopoly in the provision of airport services in major areas of the United Kingdom and it is desirable that its published accounts should, as at present, show the overall subsidisation of traffic operations by commercial activities, the cross-subsidisation within each airport and the subsidisation of one airport by another.

7.61. Having said that, we recognise that the allocation of a substantial part of the Authority's expenditure to particular activities and airports must by its nature be subject to an element of subjective judgment. In order to distinguish the results of activities before taking such expenditure into account from the results on a full cost absorption basis, we further recommend that the Authority changes the form in which it publishes its results for activities at each airport. These should show, first, the contribution made by each activity at each airport, after deducting only direct expenditure and indirect expenditure which can be attributed with reasonable accuracy to that activity ('specific expenditure'), making full use of the 'general ledger' system. From that contribution there should then be deducted an appropriate allocation of general overhead expenses ('non-specific expenditure'), made according to the Authority's best judgment and accompanied by a note explaining in some detail the basis used. This would carry through into the Authority's published results the principles already adopted for some of its management accounting reports, although with the greater degree of precision made possible by the new 'general ledger' system. The contribution made by each activity would thus be stated with an acceptable degree of accuracy and the extent to which the published results of activities are dependent on the use of judgment to allocate non-specific expenditure would also be made clear.

7.62. Our final recommendations in this chapter concern BAA's internal audit function, which we consider is important in encouraging the efficient use of its resources. While we have no reason to believe that posts in the internal audit branch, including that of the CIA, are not correctly graded, we hope that the Authority will keep this matter under careful review. The grading of internal audit staff should be fully commensurate with their responsibilities and at a level at which they can fulfil their duties effectively and carry appropriate weight in discussions with operational managers whose work they are examining and with whom they are required to follow up the implementation of their recommendations.

7.63. We found the general organisation and operation of the internal audit function to be satisfactory (although response times were tending to lengthen) and the specimen reports that we examined were evidence of the thoroughness of the examinations that had been carried out. However, the effectiveness of the internal audit function depends not only on the existence of a sound organisational structure but also on continued full support being given by the Managing Director and senior management. We therefore consider it desirable that the CIA should report directly to a member of the main Board of the Authority who should exercise close supervision over the internal audit work. We think that the Audit Committee should become more closely involved and in particular that its functions include approval of the audit programme. This programme should be more extensive, in particular by including more concessions. The Audit Committee should monitor progress and oversee the extent to which there is effective and timely compliance with the internal auditors' recommendations.

CHAPTER 8

Capital expenditure

Capital expenditure

8.1. BAA estimates that about 30 per cent of capital expenditure from 1976–77 to 1983–84 was on commercial activities. The estimates are given in Table 8.1.

TABLE 8.1 **Estimated analysis of capital additions***

			£ million
	Traffic	*Commercial*	*Total*
1976–77	20·26	10·87	31·13
1977–78	43·51	21·23	64·74
1978–79	13·78	5·94	19·72
1979–80	28·49	12·19	40·67
1980–81	48·43	16·88	65·31
1981–82	31·11	16·93	48·04
1982–83	53·19	21·75	74·94
1983–84	37·77	14·04	51·81
Total (out-turn price)	276·54	119·84	396·36

Source: BAA.

*Excluding Head Office and assets not yet brought into use such as Heathrow Terminal 4.

Investment in commercial activities averaged about £15 million per annum at out-turn prices over the last eight years, and £21 million at 1983–84 prices. About one-third of this expenditure represents an allocation of common costs (for example heating and air conditioning plant, and main services such as roads, drainage and telephones). Some of these costs are unlikely to vary in proportion to the space provided for commercial activities. Rented accommodation accounts for about two-thirds of the assets allocated to commercial activities, the balance being accounted for by concessions.

8.2. From information provided by BAA about investment projects completed in 1982–83, it is estimated that investment in property projects accounted for about half of commercial investment completed in that year, and investment in projects relating specifically to concessions for less than one-fifth. The remaining expenditure was in large combined projects, for example the Gatwick Satellite, which provided expansion of both traffic and associated commercial facilities. Major terminal developments account for a more significant part of current investment. In 1984–85 expenditure on Heathrow Terminal 4 and Gatwick North Terminal amounted to about 70 per cent of BAA investment expenditure; investment in the commercial element of such major terminal developments at present accounts for most investment in commercial facilities.

75

Procedures for dealing with capital expenditure proposals

8.3. BAA states that, as a nationalised industry, it has regard to Government guidelines on the undertaking of financial appraisals, and in particular to advice received from the sponsoring department (the Department of Transport) which normally concerns itself only with appraisals covering major capital expenditure. Projects of over £15 million at Heathrow and Gatwick and £5 million elsewhere are submitted formally for approval to the Department, which in turn seeks Treasury consent for expenditure over £50 million. In order to ensure the achievement of an overall rate of return of 5 per cent as required by Cmnd 7131,[1] the Government seeks an initial estimated return of 7 per cent as a 'margin for risk and appraisal optimism'. Departments have also requested that appraisals of major projects show the effect of excluding duty-free revenues, on the grounds that this may be an anomaly in the market, rather than an economic benefit of air travel. The Department of Transport has also recently begun to examine the appraisal of a sample of smaller capital projects.

8.4. Within BAA, the level at which capital projects are approved depends principally on project size. Projects of over £5 million require full Board approval. Below that level, the power to approve capital expenditure is delegated to the Managing Director. He in turn allows an Airport Director discretion to deal with capital projects of up to £1 million, and an Airport Director also has powers to delegate.

8.5. BAA policy is to require a financial appraisal for all airport works in excess of £30,000, the limit having recently been lowered from £100,000. Cash flow forecasts are required and appropriate discount rates are applied, although prior to 1985 there was no official appraisal manual, but the Authority followed the official Treasury guidelines. For projects required on grounds other than financial viability—primarily safety, security and passenger service—the other grounds of approval are reported.

8.6. In 1978, in response to Cmnd 7131, BAA adopted three main discount rates, all based on the Government requirement to achieve a 5 per cent return on all new investment. The 5 per cent rate was to be used for comparing best techniques for obtaining a given output, as indicated in the White Paper. For profit-making investments, the base cost of capital was increased to allow for risk and appraisal optimism, and to provide a margin to cover non-revenue earning investments; a rate of 10 per cent was to be used for traffic-related and 8 per cent for 'safer' property-related projects. Recent revisions in the guidelines for project assessment and in the use of test discount rates are discussed in paragraphs 8.15 to 8.17.

Case studies of investment in commercial facilities

8.7. We examined the appraisals of investments in 26 specific commercial facilities, ranging in size from £40,000 to £4 million. The net present value, or in some cases the internal rate of return, was quantified for 17 of them. In four cases the investment was undertaken even though the rate of return was below the prevailing test discount rate. Two projects at Gatwick—the early phases of the cargo development and the £2 million North Roof office block—and the

[1]Cmnd 7131, 'The Nationalised Industries', March 1978.

provision of a transit shed at Stansted were justified by the need to provide facilities in order to attract traffic to these airports. For the fourth project—expansion of the Gatwick multi-storey car park in 1978—the rate of return would have exceeded the test discount rate had the project been deferred, but early expansion was justified by a projected underspend on capital budget, and the probability of restrictions on capital expenditure in later years.

8.8. No formal appraisal appears to have been undertaken for the remaining nine projects. Three of these, however, were justified by the rapid payback expected. In one case, the Authority was guaranteed additional annual income equivalent to the amount of capital expenditure incurred; but in another—the expansion of the Gatwick duty-free shop—the rate of payback was exaggerated by BAA.[1] Of the remaining six cases, one catering project was justified by the requirement to improve service, and two car park schemes—at Edinburgh and Stansted—by the general obligation to provide facilities. In the case of two projects—provision of improved bonded store facilities at Heathrow Terminal 3 and at Glasgow—the benefits were regarded as unquantifiable, though some assessment had been undertaken of a similar scheme. The justification for the final project—a buffet in the domestic arrivals area at Heathrow Terminal 1—cannot be traced; subsequent assessment suggests a rate of above 10 per cent.

8.9. Only a minority of appraisals contained sensitivity analyses, or discussion of a range of alternative options.

'Combined' projects

8.10. We examined the appraisal of investment in six 'combined' projects, primarily traffic facilities, but also including associated commercial facilities. The projects range from a £660,000 investment in passenger facilities at Aberdeen to the £200 million development of the Gatwick North Terminal: some 20 per cent of the latter is attributable to commercial facilities.

8.11. All six projects were subject to formal investment appraisal. Appraisals of the larger projects also incorporated extensive sensitivity analysis, or direct risk analysis using a computerised 'Monte Carlo' method[2]. The return on the major schemes—the Gatwick North Terminal, and Terminal 4 at Heathrow—was estimated at somewhat less than the 10 per cent normally required by the Authority of traffic-related investments; but BAA believed that the sensitivity and risk analyses undertaken showed a sufficient probability that the rate of return would exceed the 5 per cent required by the Government. The appraisals generally presented only a limited range of options; BAA told us that, in consequence of the system of public inquiry into its planning applications, these options were mainly concerned with phasing. Our interest in these projects, however, has primarily concerned the appraisal of those aspects of the investment relating to the provision of commercial facilities.

8.12. The returns on five of the projects are highly dependent, at projected levels of traffic income, on the generation of commercial revenues; but the projects were only appraised as a whole, with no separate appraisal of individual

---

[1] We have since been told that payback was in fact completed in 18 months.

[2] This method calculates the outcomes of the investment appraisal for a large number of cases (typically 1,000) by sampling values for the key assumptions.

F

commercial elements, or of options for providing commercial facilities. In the sixth case, the expansion of passenger facilities at Aberdeen, the return on the investment in concessions fell short of the return required but was justified on service grounds. Provision of space for commercial activities in the design of new terminal facilities is based initially on BAA's planning guidelines (see paragraph 5.25 *et seq*), adjusted to take advantage of the potential for increased commercial revenues. BAA also told us that the options for provision of commercial facilities in recent projects have been constrained by the nature of the sites available.

8.13. The three most recent major developments at the South-East airports provide additional commercial facilities, compared with existing terminal buildings. The increases in commercial revenues assumed in the appraisals of these developments varied:

(a) The appraisal of the Heathrow Terminal 4 development in 1981 assumed a 25 per cent increase in duty- and tax-free income per passenger above 1980–81 levels, resulting from the provision of better facilities, with no real increase from other concession activities.

(b) The appraisal of the North Terminal development at Gatwick in 1983 was based on average South-East concession income per passenger. This represented a small increase on average income at Gatwick on the assumption that traffic using the terminal would consist of existing Heathrow services and some present Gatwick scheduled passengers. Despite the provision of a significantly larger duty- and tax-free shop, in relation to the traffic volume to be handled, than in the existing terminal, no allowance was made for further increasing the potential level of commercial income. BAA now believes this assumption was conservative.

(c) The recent appraisal of the proposed redevelopment of Terminal 3 at Heathrow assumed a 30 per cent increase in duty- and tax-free income per IDP, and an 18 per cent increase in other concession income per passenger. It was assumed, for example, that provision of a larger duty- and tax-free shop would increase the range of goods to be sold and increase penetration of the market for tax-free sales by 50 per cent; but it was acknowledged that this assumption was somewhat subjective.

The assumptions of increased income in the two Heathrow projects reflect BAA's belief that shortage of space in the existing Heathrow terminals is a constraint on the maximisation of commercial income. Gatwick's South Terminal was not at that time considered to suffer from this constraint to the same extent.

8.14. BAA subsequently estimated the marginal costs (including the opportunity cost of capital) and revenues of providing commercial facilities at Heathrow Terminal 4 and the Gatwick North Terminal, as part of a collaborative study of landing charges with a number of international airlines. This information is summarised in Table 8.2. These estimates would appear to confirm that investment in the commercial facilities of these projects, in particular in duty- and tax-free facilities, is likely to be profitable, but no appraisal has been carried out of the return on investment in specific facilities other than duty-free shops.

TABLE 8.2 **Estimated costs and revenues per international passenger of provision of commercial facilities** (March 1983 prices)

£

	Heathrow Terminal 4			Gatwick North Terminal		
	Duty-free	Other commercial	Total	Duty-free	Other commercial	Total
Costs per passenger	0·11	1·08	1·19	0·11	1·21	1·32
Revenues per passenger	1·54	1·64	3·18	1·27	1·32	2·59
Net revenue per passenger	1·43	0·56	1·99	1·16	0·11	1·27

Source: BAA.

Revised guidelines on project appraisal

8.15. BAA has recently reviewed its methods for financial appraisal. New ' Policy Guidelines on Project Assessment' were approved by the Board in April 1985; in addition a financial Appraisal Manual has been prepared giving details of a standard approach for use throughout BAA. Among the main features of the guidelines are:

(a) A more flexible use of test discount rates is to be adopted, to provide for varied levels of risk. Eight different types of project are described, with six different discount rates ranging from 5 per cent for ' fixed contracts with guarantees' to 20 per cent for ' highly speculative one-off projects '.

(b) It is BAA policy that all airport works above £30,000 (previously £100,000) should be subject to formal financial appraisal, and that remaining small projects should also require justification, though possibly using less rigorous approaches.

(c) Financial departments should undertake back-checks to review the appropriateness and success of forecasting and other methods used in past appraisals.

(d) Project appraisals require a sensitivity analysis to evaluate how robust are the overall results of the appraisal, and to indicate which assumptions are the most important in determining the result. Additionally, it is intended that direct risk analysis be carried out on all future major projects, using the base cost of capital (5 per cent), and financial appraisals be carried out for alternative options.

(e) For service projects from which no profits are sought, it is acknowledged that standard financial appraisals cannot be applied in full; but appraisals should be performed of alternative methods of achieving a particular service standard; or an evaluation undertaken of the cost and financial impact of the project. In certain cases (largely traffic investments such as provision of a taxiway turnoff) preliminary cost benefit analysis should be undertaken.

79

8.16. On two specific areas of commercial investment:

(a) It is recommended in the guidelines that property projects should generally not be carried out if market rents fall short of ' economic ' rents, ie the rents necessary to earn an adequate return on the investment.

(b) The treatment of catering projects is acknowledged to be difficult. BAA regards a basic catering provision as an essential passenger service and the Board has laid down that a profit margin of 1 to 2 per cent, although insufficient to provide the required return on new investment, is adequate for service-related projects. BAA is discussing a definition of essential catering facilities, to be appraised as passenger service projects, with optional projects meeting normal criteria (usually a 10 per cent return).

8.17. In order to monitor the application of these guidelines, copies of the financial appraisals for all projects approved under Directors' delegated powers are to be submitted to Head Office. Airport Directors are also to monitor the application of the guidelines to projects between £30,000 and £100,000.

Back-checks

8.18. There has not previously been a systematic programme of back-checks on investment decisions, although a number of back-checks have been carried out on particular projects. The Finance Economics branch at Head Office has recently set itself a target of completing six back-checks per year of sizeable projects. The Finance Department at Heathrow also carries out a substantial number of back-checks.

Arrangements for monitoring of investment expenditure

8.19. Consolidated quarterly returns are prepared for the Managing Director showing all new capital projects authorised at values between £100,000 and £5 million, all uncompleted capital projects showing original authorised costs and forecast out-turn (at constant prices), and all capital projects completed in the quarter showing original authorised costs and forecast out-turn (at constant prices).

8.20. If the forecast out-turn for any project varies by more than ± 10 per cent of the authorised cost, the report must be accompanied by an explanation of the forecast variance. Board approval is required for increases in excess of £500,000 above the cost of projects approved by the Board. It should be noted, however, that the authorised cost includes an allowance of 5 to 10 per cent for contingencies. For smaller projects, therefore, a total variance of up to + 20 per cent is allowed before the reasons for cost increases have to be reported.

Conclusions

8.21. Our examination of the appraisal of a number of investment projects indicates that the majority of investments have been subject to formal investment appraisal. The recent adoption of revised guidelines for project assessment should, however, lead to some improvement in the techniques of investment appraisal, particularly as applied to smaller projects.

8.22. In particular, the standard of investment appraisal should benefit from a wider quantification of available options; from a greater use of sensitivity analysis; from a more systematic assessment of non-financial benefits; and from a regular programme of back-checks as proposed in the revised guidelines.

8.23. No separate appraisal is carried out of the commercial content of the major 'combined' investments. BAA argued that options for provision of commercial facilities have been constrained by the nature of the sites available. We believe this argument can be overstated. Where there are options for the provision of commercial facilities in these major developments, these options also should be subjected to a formal economic appraisal.

CHAPTER 9

Concessions and licences

9.1. At each of its airports BAA grants rights (generally known as concessions) for the sale of goods and services to the public and similar rights (generally known as licences) for sales to airlines.[1]

The market for concessions

9.2. Table 9.1 sets out the principal areas of concession income for BAA in the year ending March 1985. Figures for earlier years are shown in Table 7.5.

TABLE 9.1   **BAA concession income, 1984–85**

	£ million
Duty-free liquor	25·6
Duty-free tobacco products	18·1
Other tax-free	25·4
Tax- and duty-paid goods	10·1
Catering	6·3
Advertising	1·9
Car hire	5·2
Car parking	16·3
Other concession income (including banking)	11·0
Advertising administered by concessionaires	(1·0)
Total all concessions	118·9

Source: BAA.

9.3. The concessions are usually offered for tender on a terminal by terminal basis, but at some airports the facilities may be combined under one concession agreement. For example, at Stansted the duty-free, tax-free and duty-paid shops are operated as one concession in view of the low passenger throughput. Car hire concessions are granted on an airport-wide basis. Table 9·2 shows the number of separate concession agreements by airport for each main area of activity.

9.4. In practice the major concessions at BAA airports are held by relatively few companies. For the duty- and tax-free shops Allders has the concession at Heathrow (all terminals) and Gatwick, with Trusthouse Forte (THF) having these concessions at the remaining five BAA airports. THF also holds the concessions for the duty-paid Skyshops at all BAA airports except Edinburgh. The catering concessions (all terminals) at Heathrow and Glasgow are held by THF, the concessionaire at Gatwick and Edinburgh is J L Catering, whilst the concessions at Stansted (since April 1985), Prestwick and Aberdeen are held by Sports and Leisure Foods.

9.5. On car hire the position is similar, with three main companies having the majority of the airport concessions. Avis and Hertz are concessionaires at six of

---

[1]We deal with licences to occupy property in Chapter 10.

TABLE 9.2   Number of separate concession agreements at BAA airports

	Heathrow	Gatwick	Stansted	Glasgow	Edinburgh	Prestwick	Aberdeen
Shops—duty-free liquor and tobacco	3	1		1	1	1	1
Shops—tax-free			1				
Principal duty-paid shops (Skyshops*)	5	1		1	1	1	1
Other duty-paid shops†	16	2	—	1	—	—	—
Public catering	3	1	1	1	1	1	1
Car hire	4	4	1	3	4	3	4
Car parking	1	1	none‡	1	1	1	1
Banking	3	2	1	1	1	1	1

Source: BAA.

* Skyshops are described in paragraph 4.3.
† Specialist retail outlets.
‡ BAA operates the car parking facilities at Stansted.
Note: The advertising concession for all BAA airports is held by More O'Ferrall on a single contract.

BAA's seven airports whilst Godfrey Davis Europcar are concession holders at five. Swan National, Kennings and Budget share the remaining six concessions.

9.6.   NCP operates all public car parks at the BAA airports except at Stansted, where BAA is the operator.

9.7.   For comparison, Table 9.3 shows the holders of the various concessions at each of the six largest local authority airports. The position is essentially similar to that at BAA airports, with a limited number of companies holding the concessions.

Contracts with concessionaires

9.8.   In most cases the form of contract between BAA and a concessionaire specifies an agreement period of five years.[1] In certain cases an option to extend the contract for a further three years exists. BAA told us that extensions would now only be granted in exceptional circumstances, for example if BAA required the concessionaires' co-operation in redevelopment, or where because of redevelopment or for other reasons trading had been interrupted for a time during the contract period. On extension terms are renegotiated with the concessionaire.

9.9.   BAA said that the length of the initial contract was a balance between the needs to maintain competition by tendering at regular intervals, and to provide stability and an opportunity for the concessionaire to develop his business. It was BAA policy not to encourage major investment by concessionaires, who under the contracts would only be responsible for minor capital items such as tills and cutlery. BAA undertook all other investment in fixtures and fittings because it

[1]The current car hire contracts at Heathrow were let in April 1985 for three years, because of uncertainties in operation likely to be caused by the opening of Terminal 4.

Table 9.3 **Concessionaires at local authority airports**

	Newcastle	Luton	Leeds/Bradford	Manchester	Birmingham	East Midlands
Duty-free and tax-free	Finnigans	Allders	Trusthouse Forte	Trusthouse Forte	Trusthouse Forte	Fenton Hill International
Duty-paid*	John Menzies	Trusthouse Forte	Trusthouse Forte	W H Smith	W H Smith	Midport Stores
Catering	Trusthouse Forte	Trusthouse Forte	Trusthouse Forte	SAS	Trusthouse Forte	Sports and Leisure Foods
Car hire	Avis, Hertz	Avis, Swan	Avis, Hertz, Godfrey Davis Europcar	Avis, Hertz, Godfrey Davis Europcar Local authority	Avis, Hertz, Godfrey Davis Europcar	Avis, Hertz, Godfrey Davis Europcar
Car parking	NCP	Local authority	NCP		NCP	NCP
Advertising	W H Smith	W H Smith	W H Smith	More O'Ferrall	W H Smith	W H Smith

Sources: Local authorities.

* Principal duty-paid shop. Other specialist shops also operate.

84

considered that if concessionaires were responsible for major investment, difficulties would be experienced when contracts expired. BAA also told us that capital participation by concessionaires would inevitably require a longer-term contract to enable the concessionaire to recover his initial investment. Moreover, he would be unwilling to incur any further expenditure on necessary alterations, particularly near the end of the contract term, unless an extension was granted, and would therefore not respond to changing market demands. In BAA's view these considerations justified limiting the contract term to five years without major capital participation by concessionaires.

9.10. THF told us that it believed that there would be considerable merit in longer and less restrictive contracts with the opportunity for capital investment. The concessionaire could then take a longer-term view and could achieve a higher level of service and sales performance through his own management expertise. He could also respond more readily to changes in the market. THF thought this would enable the concessionaire to participate in the design of facilities to meet market requirements; and that capital investment by the concessionaire would encourage a higher standard of service because of his need to ensure a good return.

9.11. The Board of BAA considered that if catering concessionaires were to undertake capital investment the problems would outweigh the advantages. The Board nevertheless recognised the merit of a performance-related incentive. To this end BAA has relaxed the overall degree of price control on catering concessions (see paragraph 11.12 *et seq*) and intends to introduce an incentive scheme on an experimental basis, which if successful may be extended to other commercial activities.

9.12. Some of the concession agreements at local authority airports are for a longer period than those at BAA airports, commonly for five to seven years. Some local authority airports have agreements for periods of up to 21 years, usually dating back to the late 1960s, which have proved unsatisfactory in that it is difficult for airport operators to ensure appropriate responses to changes in passenger mix and pattern of demand. It is also more common to find capital participation by concessionaires at these airports.

9.13. Allders told us that longer contracts would offer better career paths to middle management. A further problem was that the normal five-year concession contract did not match the typical 21-year lease for the necessary back-up warehouse.

9.14. BAA considered that many of the staffing problems which concessionaires have would be associated with any contract of finite length. Recognising these problems it sought to encourage tenderers to employ the staff of the existing concessionaire, although this requirement was not included in contract agreements.

9.15. Concessionaires are usually required to pay BAA a fixed percentage of turnover (exclusive of VAT). The agreements relating to duty- and tax-free goods initially specify a percentage of turnover, but allow BAA subsequently to vary this in response to changes in the cost price of the goods sold. In car hire the percentage payment is subject to a minimum guarantee. Otherwise minimum guarantees are generally only applied when a new type of concession is tried as a marketing experiment, often for a short term of six to nine months. The minimum guarantee in such cases is based on the expected income from alternative uses. The terms for banking concessions are described in paragraph 4.5.

9.16. Table 9.4 shows the average percentage of concessionaires' turnover accruing to BAA in respect of the principal concession activities. Tenderers for the duty-free, tax-free, duty-paid and catering contracts are required to bid a percentage of turnover for each of many specified product lines within the broad categories shown in the table. Thus, for example, a prospective duty-free concessionaire would be required to provide a range of bids covering some 20 product groups.

TABLE 9.4 **BAA concession income as a percentage of concessionaires' turnover, 1983–84**

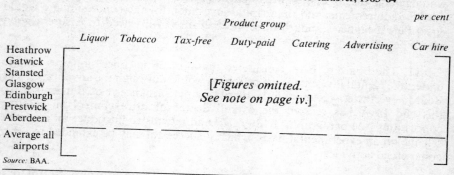

| | Product group | | | | | | per cent |
	Liquor	Tobacco	Tax-free	Duty-paid	Catering	Advertising	Car hire
Heathrow							
Gatwick							
Stansted							
Glasgow			*[Figures omitted.*				
Edinburgh			*See note on page iv.]*				
Prestwick							
Aberdeen							
Average all airports							

Source: BAA.

Note: The broad categories shown cover many individual product groups and the percentages shown are thus the average across these groups.

9.17. The percentages shown in Table 9.4 are significantly higher than those which we found at local authority airports.

9.18. In general concessionaires are controlled by their agreements in their pricing, product specification and range, and matters such as promotion, opening hours, staff numbers etc. The pricing policy of BAA and the principal conditions contained in the contracts are discussed in Chapter 11.

Licences

9.19. Services to airlines (see paragraph 4.6 *et seq*) can be provided by:

(a) other airlines;

(b) third parties operating on the airport;

(c) third parties operating off the airport; or

(d) directly by BAA.

The detailed arrangements vary considerably between airports; some of them are considered in detail in Chapter 11. Tables 11.1 to 11.3 show the provision of the principal services by terminal at Heathrow.

9.20. BAA derives income from these services in four ways:

(a) For services provided by airlines it charges for the use of facilities such as check-in desks. The exception to this is any handling business at Heathrow gained by Aer Lingus since January 1984, for which a fee of [*] per cent is prescribed (but see paragraph 11.49).

(b) For services provided by other on-airport agents BAA charges a percentage of turnover as a licence fee (for example Gatwick Handling— see paragraph 11.57—pays [*] per cent on all its business) together with rent for the use of facilities.The arrangements are in some cases embodied in a lease.

(c) Off-airport operators are charged a percentage of turnover (or a fixed annual sum if the volume of business is small) as a licence fee.

(d) It makes a direct charge to airlines for services which it provides itself. Such services are outside our terms of reference.

Thus not all the income from the supply of services to airlines arises as licence fees to BAA. Table 9.5 shows BAA's licence fee income for 1983–84.

TABLE 9.5 **BAA income from ground handling-related licence fees, 1983–84**

£'000

	Heathrow	Gatwick	Stansted	Glasgow	Aberdeen	Prestwick	Edinburgh
In-flight catering	*	*	*	*	*	*	*
Baggage and aircraft handling and cleaning	*	*	*	*	*		
Aircrew transport	*	*	*				
Trucked aircargo/ transit sheds	*	*		*	*		*
Other	*				*		

Source: BAA.

Note: This table does not include income from services provided by BAA to airlines, which are outside our terms of reference.

9.21. Licence agreements are usually for a period of three years subject to six months' notice by either party. Typical terms are [*] per cent of turnover with a minimum guaranteed payment per annum to BAA. Other clauses limit the licensee to supplying only specified services to specified airlines. It is a condition that licences are only granted subject to airside contracts being obtained by the licensee.

9.22. BAA told us that it seeks to limit the provision of airside licences and that new licences would only be granted after receiving representations from airlines (at Heathrow and Gatwick from the respective Airline Operators Committee). Licences are not offered for tender but follow from the nominations of the airlines which themselves are often suppliers of the particular services and as such are in competition with off-airport operators. By contrast at Manchester airport (a local authority airport) we were told that when airlines had requested further in-flight caterers the licence had been put out to tender.

* Figures omitted. See note on page iv.

Conclusions

9.23. The existing concession period of five years appears to give rise to some disadvantages to concessionaires. This short period may make it difficult to attract and retain good staff and management, and is inconsistent with any major capital investment by concessionaires. We received conflicting views as to the benefits of such investment, particularly in respect of catering. BAA said that if the concessionaire had made a major investment, he would, with a fixed contract length, be reluctant to re-invest particularly near the end of the contract. THF told us that such investment would lead to greater responsiveness to the market and provide a significant incentive to the concessionaire to maintain service and sales performance.

9.24. While five-year contracts may not be in the best interests of the concessionaires, given the nature of the monopoly rights granted by BAA we think that all contracts should remain subject to regular tendering. We consider that this question of capital investment by catering concessionaires should be kept under review in the light of the outcome of BAA's recent proposals to provide them with a greater incentive.

CHAPTER 10

Rents and property

10.1. Property accounts for about two-thirds of the assets invested in BAA's commercial facilities. Rents of £24·8 million accounted in 1983–84 for about 8 per cent of BAA's income, and 17 per cent of its non-traffic income. Income from 'services'—primarily on-charges to tenants for utilities such as space heating and electricity—amounted to a further £25 million. Seventy-two per cent of 'rents and services' income is generated at Heathrow, and a further 17 per cent at Gatwick.

10.2. Property lettings are distinguished from trading concessions by the form of grant to the occupier, and the way in which the rent or fee is calculated. There are four main types of grant:

(a) *Licences* are used for check-in and for other types of desks within the terminals, giving BAA as landlord the flexibility to move desks to meet changing demand; licences are also used for a range of miscellaneous grants.

(b) *Short-term tenancies* account for most transactions; they cover grants of floor space at rack rents for uses such as offices, pier accommodation and warehouses, and are also used for short-term purposes. Length of term varies from indeterminate up to about five years. Tenants cannot use the let property except for the narrow purpose specified, and in general cannot assign or sub-let.

(c) *Long leases* are granted at rack rents for terms of more than five years. They are fairly few in number.

(d) *Ground leases* are usually granted in conjunction with building agreements for the lessee to fund the building or other works which will be for his own occupation. The length of the ground lease has to be adequate for investment by the lessee and varies from 21 to 125 years. Some of the more substantial airport developments have been provided under this type of grant, for example maintenance bases, warehouses, office blocks, flight catering bases, fuel farms and hydrants. In general, sub-letting is prohibited but assignment is permitted subject to consent by BAA. As an alternative to consent, most assignment clauses give BAA the right to buy back the lease at current market value. In Scotland most leases prohibit sub-letting and assignment.

10.3. With some exceptions payment to BAA is at a fixed annual sum and not, as with concessions, a percentage of the occupier's turnover. Main exceptions, however, include a recent office development on Northside at Heathrow, where payment was a cash premium plus a percentage of rack rents; five airport hotels with payments calculated as a proportion of turnover; and the fuel supply at Heathrow, discussed in paragraphs 10.23 to 10.26. Care is taken not to grant a tenancy at a fixed rent for an activity which could be subject to a concession.

Objectives and policies

10.4. BAA has four main objectives in the leasing of property:

(a) furtherance of its statutory duty ' to provide at its aerodromes such services and facilities as are in its opinion necessary or desirable for their operation ';

(b) optimisation of the use of all accommodation including land;

(c) maximisation of rents; and

(d) in appropriate cases, for lessees to fund provision of facilities.

10.5. BAA interprets its statutory duty as preventing it from investing in activities not related to an airport and from letting property in central areas for such activities. Joint ventures in any case require permission from the Government, which has been refused several times. BAA allocates accommodation only to companies which have a definite civil aviation and airport connection, and for a specified use. When supply of accommodation exceeds demand, however, this policy has been relaxed for short-term tenancies.

The leasing/renting process

10.6. Commission staff have discussed the process of leasing and renting property with Head Office and airport property staff. Examination of files at Gatwick, Heathrow and Glasgow airports showed that both the policies of BAA discussed above and the formal processes established by Head Office were being followed.

Utilisation of property

10.7. Some office accommodation has become vacant at Heathrow, where some 44,000 square feet of BAA office accommodation was unlet in August 1984, plus a further 38,000 square feet at a privately financed development on Northside (see paragraph 10.3). This resulted from the recent recession and in particular the retrenchment by British Airways. The rental value of BAA unlet accommodation was estimated by BAA at £490,000 per annum, but with some further loss of income to BAA through voids on the Northside development. BAA projections summarised in Table 10.1 suggest that the amount of unlet accommodation is likely to increase with the opening of Heathrow Terminal 4 (because airlines transferring there will release accommodation in the central area). BAA expects supply and demand to be back in balance by 1989–90, though still with some mis-match between terminals.

10.8. A significant proportion of the spare accommodation foreseen in the central area is in Terminal 3 and Queens Building. BAA told us that it is necessary for some of the accommodation in Terminal 3 to be held vacant in order to close down areas of the terminal for redevelopment, and that it is safeguarding accommodation in Queens Building for potential moves of airlines into Terminal 1. Allowing for these factors, the amount of vacant accommodation is relatively limited compared with the total amount of office

TABLE 10.1 **Overall supply and demand for office accommodation, Heathrow**

						square feet	
		1984–85	*1985–86*	*1986–87*	*1987–88*	*1988–89*	*1989–90*
Terminals 1–4	Supply	31,200	132,200	153,000	153,000	153,000	153,000
and central Area	Demand	5,200	78,200	105,800	129,800	139,800	149,800
	Excess supply	26,000	54,000	47,200	23,200	13,200	3,200
Northside,	Supply	69,700	69,700	75,700	75,700	75,700	75,700
cargo and other	Demand	15,400	32,000	39,000	56,000	73,000	90,000
areas	Excess supply	54,300	37,700	36,700	19,700	2,700	− 14,300

Source: BAA.

Note: Projections take no account of possible new developments, but only of possible increases in demand. ' Northside ' includes the privately financed development at Cardinal Point.

accommodation at Heathrow (about 1 million square feet), and BAA considers it not far out of line with vacancies resulting from normal turnover in tenancies.

10.9. However, in response to the temporary excess supply of office accommodation at Heathrow, BAA has relaxed its letting policy in the central area to allow a wider range of organisations to take short-term 'contracted out'[1] tenancies. This enables the Authority to restore its basic letting policy when the market recovers. Lettings totalling approximately 4,200 square feet were granted in 1983 in Terminal 2 and Queens Building to organisations such as a building society, a business centre, Diners Club and a solicitor's practice. In non-sensitive areas outside terminals, positive steps have been taken to market accommodation to a wider range of organisations. As a result, a number of lettings have been made in peripheral areas to non-aviation companies.

10.10. At Gatwick, BAA has provided office accommodation in line with traffic forecasts of growth in demand at the airport. Following the recent recession, a number of carriers either ceased service at Gatwick, for example Pan Am and Transworld, or went out of business, eg Laker and Braniff. The reletting of accommodation was difficult until the recent recovery of growth in North Atlantic traffic. During 1984–85 the amount of unlet office space decreased from 44,000 to 29,000 square feet (from 20 per cent to 13 per cent of the total), though a large part of this reduction is accounted for by the allocation of space to BAA Head Office staff. A further 3,000 square feet of accommodation have recently been let, and half of the remainder is under offer; the balance (nearly 6 per cent of the total) is all that remains available until the North Terminal opens. As at Heathrow, a number of short-term lettings have been made to non-aviation activities.

10.11. Landside accommodation at the Scottish airports is advertised when supply exceeds demand; to maintain a high occupancy rate companies are offered short-term tenancies, in some cases at reduced rents.

10.12. There is significant under-utilisation of cargo facilities constructed by the airlines on ground lease at Heathrow. BAA cannot re-allocate those sheds where capacity is under-utilised, and is therefore having to consider the

[1]That is, from the provisions of the Landlord and Tenant Act 1954.

construction of extra cargo facilities to meet new demand. BAA has told us that it is prepared to relax user clause restrictions if better use of facilities results. It has, for example, permitted trucking to and from the transit sheds at Heathrow and in certain cases has relaxed the prohibition on sub-letting in return for payments negotiated with the ground lessees having regard to the value of the space sub-let.

10.13. British Airways told us that the restrictive conditions in leases and tenancies discourage the best use of land and buildings, and do not allow airlines to exploit their business to the full by maximising the use of property assets. It quoted a particular example where the Authority requested an additional rent of £30,000 per annum to allow sub-letting of surplus hangar space. The Authority argued that this hangar was part of premises held by British Airways under an old ground lease, and that British Airways enjoys a large profit rent on this lease with rents payable to the Authority of about £500 per annum, compared with current market value of over £30,000 per annum. Since British Airways wished to be released from the restriction of certain terms so as to benefit financially, the Authority believed that it was reasonable, and usual in the circumstances, for the landlord to seek some benefit from the granting of consent. BAA told us that it was willing to approve the sub-letting of other areas, subject to payment of an appropriate consideration.

Rents

10.14. BAA policy is to charge:

(*a*) Open market rents for existing accommodation.

(*b*) Either the open market or the economic rent (the rent necessary to give an adequate return on investment in a property project including the notional cost of land), whichever is the higher, for new accommodation. This means that where the rents necessary to earn an adequate return on an investment are in excess of market rents BAA will seek an appropriate agreement prior to construction. An example of this approach was the British Caledonian transit shed extension at Heathrow.

(*c*) Open market rents for ground leases and long leases, subject to arbitration at review.

(*d*) Hybrid rents, being a ground rent with an element linked to turnover.

Charges for licences for facilities such as check-in desks are based on the costs incurred in providing and maintaining the facility plus the cost of the space used.

10.15. The policy of charging market rents at Heathrow was challenged by BOAC and BEA before the Select Committee on Nationalised Industries, 1970–71. The Authority argued that the policy followed the definition of the Landlord and Tenant Act 1954, market rent being the rent at which 'the holding might reasonably be expected to be let in the open market by a willing lessor', and that as space is short at the airport

the policy of open market rents is a useful sanction in preventing tenants taking more accommodation than they need. . . . If a tenant turned down an offer of accommodation because the rent was more than he was prepared to pay, another tenant could in general be found at the quoted rate.

92

This response was accepted without adverse comment by the Select Committee; in practice applicants entered into negotiation with BAA.

10.16. Main factors in determining open market rents include rents at which similar accommodation has been recently let; allowance for characteristics of the property; and evidence of trends in supply and demand for accommodation within the airport, and generally. For reviews on the expiry of a tenancy, the rent if disputed can be determined by the Courts under the Landlord and Tenant Act 1954 (see footnote to paragraph 4.11). In practice, although BAA has had many references to the Courts, all these have been settled by agreement. Rent reviews during the term of a tenancy are subject to private arbitration.

10.17. It is BAA policy to review rents as frequently as possible so that they are kept up to date both for inflation and for any real growth in market value. Reviews of rack rents are usually at not less than three years and licence fees for desks are usually reviewed every two years. A number of ground leases inherited by BAA in 1966, however, have long fixed terms without rent reviews, or with infrequent reviews to fixed amounts. The rental payments on these leases are considerably below current market values; an example is mentioned in paragraph 10.13. Modern ground leases have provision for frequent review—with reference, for example, to open market value of land or premises—and for arbitration in the event of dispute.

10.18. The Board does not request or receive formal submissions on rental performance compared with off-airport trends. It agrees an overall target for rental growth, and targets for each airport are settled by the Managing Director (see paragraphs 5.13 to 5.22). A review of trends in rental compared with those elsewhere in the economy was carried out for Heathrow (see paragraph 4.26) and a similar study has recently been initiated for Gatwick. BAA told us that there is constant surveillance of the off-airport market at other airports.

10.19. The detailed results of the comparative study for Heathrow mentioned above are shown in Table 10.2. Rents at Heathrow generally increased more rapidly over the period 1974 to 1983 than rents elsewhere. Increases in warehouse rents equalled or exceeded increases in the general level of prices, as measured by the Retail Price Index, and increases in the Cost of New Construction Index; but some Heathrow office rents, in common with national trends in office rentals over the period, have not kept pace with inflation. Office rents in the central terminal area at Heathrow are above those in surrounding towns (eg Staines or Slough); BAA said that this does not reflect policy but is attributable to economic market forces. British Airways, however, argued that rents and licence fees are forced up by under-provision of the facilities needed by airlines.

Investment, and disposal of property

10.20. BAA said that it does not undertake speculative development. Offices are only constructed where there is known demand or a tenant pre-signed. For development outside central areas, the Authority sometimes leases a site to allow the tenant to fund the development at his own risk. BAA needs to construct certain facilities to meet forecast growth in demand and, in the case of cargo sheds, because it cannot re-allocate existing under-used capacity. BAA also

TABLE 10.2 **Comparability of rental performance, Jan 1974 to May 1983**

Index Jan 1974 = 100

Heathrow—Offices	Index	Heathrow—warehousing	Index
Cargo terminal office block Bdgs 520	410	Bdg 139	320
Cargo agents building—Bdg 521	400	Cargo terminal—Bdg 521	320
Northside—Norwood Crescent	290	Former bonded stores building	450
Epsom Square	400		
Terminal 1 2nd floor	200		
Terminal 2 offices	280		
Terminal 3 North wing	340		

Investors Chronicle/Hillier Parker	Index		Index
All offices	170	All industrials	230
West End	140	London	240
Central London	130	South-East England	230
South-East England	210		

Retail Price Index	330
Cost of New Construction Index	300

Source: BAA.

referred to its statutory duty to provide the facilities at airports necessary for their proper operation; not all such facilities are profitable.

10.21. An internal audit report on the management of property at Heathrow criticised a previous property investment decision by the Executive for giving insufficient weight to open market rentals as advised by the professional staff. Subsequently, the Executive agreed that if market rents were lower than 'economic rents', the former should be used to establish upper limits to the capital costs of new property projects. BAA told us that the airside offices known as Building 820 were likely to be the last instance of a development where open market rents were insufficient to earn an adequate rate of return. We note that upon completion of this project there was a mis-match of supply and demand for this type of accommodation.

10.22. BAA only sells property which is surplus to requirements. There is a sale in prospect for a 1-acre plot of land in the vicinity of Heathrow, and some land may be sold at Prestwick. The Authority has identified various other parcels of land for which no precise airport-related development has been established but most of these are retained for future airport-related needs. It is BAA policy to consider the acquisition for future airport development of any sites which become available adjacent to airports.

Fuel supply at Heathrow

10.23. In August 1984 BAA entered into a new arrangement with the suppliers of aviation fuel at Heathrow; this replaced several separate arrangements with groups of oil companies formed into consortia. The fuel suppliers' turnover is estimated at between £400 and £450 million per annum. In the earlier arrangements, partly inherited by BAA and embracing some 40 agreements, oil companies leased the physical facilities needed to supply aviation fuel, and some of them also paid BAA a charge based on the quantity of fuel supplied.

10.24. The Authority told us that the leases had a common end date in 1991 and this, with the need to arrange for the supply of fuel at Terminal 4, provided a basis to re-negotiate the arrangements with the oil companies. Prominent amongst the new arrangements were the replacement of the previous rents and quantity charges by a rent indexed to RPI, with two stepped increases related to passenger growth. This resulted in a [*] increase in the payments to BAA.

10.25. The Authority was also concerned to ensure that the new long-term arrangement (21 years) did not confer an absolute monopoly on the existing nine suppliers of aviation fuel, but would allow the entry of other suitable suppliers. This was effected on the basis of the world-wide agreement between oil companies known as the Joint Users Hydrant Installation. However, this agreement allows the fuel suppliers discretion in accepting a new entrant; the Authority insisted on clauses in its arrangement which allow a potential entrant, approved by BAA, to ask the Authority to call in an arbitrator if the new consortium claims lack of technical competence. A new entrant must pay a share of the cost of the facilities. The nine fuel suppliers now established as the Heathrow Hydrant Consortium have provided us with the agreement which secures the operation of the system. Entry to the consortium is restricted to a ' marketer of aviation fuel '.

10.26. British Airways told us that it had applied for membership of the consortium but difficulties had arisen; it is now considering taking legal action against the consortium. For its part BAA has recently given British Airways permission to build and operate fuel tanks on the airport, subject to the caveat that it may be required to share those tanks with another new entrant because of the shortage of land at the airport. The particular site will initially be let for a limited term as it may be required for other airport development.

Fuel supply at Gatwick

10.27. The Authority told us that eight oil companies comprise the Gatwick Hydrant Consortium. Payment is made to BAA under leases for the facilities, and there is a quantity payment. BAA believed that the new arrangements made at Heathrow would be suitable for Gatwick. It had put this proposal to the consortium but negotiations had not yet begun, one problem being that the leases have longer to run than at Heathrow.

10.28. British Caledonian told us that costs were increased and competition reduced because each of the four companies it buys from at Gatwick has its own line to the aircraft fuelling points. It would prefer the system widely adopted in the United States where one approved agent operates a common fuel line system. This reduces costs and permits a number of oil companies to supply fuel through the common system, which increases competition between them.

---

* Figure omitted. See note on page iv.

Conclusions

10.29. Examination of files and discussions with airport staff showed that the policies and procedures for leasing were being followed in detail.

10.30. Although there is at present some vacant office accommodation at both Heathrow and Gatwick, this represents a small proportion of total office accommodation at the two airports. BAA projections suggest that the excess supply should be absorbed within five years.

10.31. The increase in rents at Heathrow airport has been greater than the national average, although some office rents at Heathrow have not kept pace with inflation. The level of rents at Heathrow is also generally above that in surrounding areas. BAA policy for determining rental levels appears reasonable.

10.32. There is provision in the new fuel agreement at Heathrow for entry of new suppliers to the hydrant consortium; it will be easier to judge the effectiveness of this provision when the result of British Airways' application to join the consortium is known. BAA should increase competition in the supply of fuel at Gatwick when the present fuel arrangements are re-negotiated.

CHAPTER 11

Competition

Sales to the public through concessions

Role of the tendering process in competition

11.1. BAA told us that competition is promoted in two ways through its present tendering processes. First, potential suppliers compete for the concession contracts; to maintain this competition contracts are let for relatively short periods, normally five years. Secondly, BAA considers that competition is increased by extending the range of goods available. In the last two years the Trading Department has introduced small specialist shops such as Tie Rack, Olympus Sports and WHS Computer Shops, and is trying to increase the variety of retailing. BAA believes that given the limitations on space in terminals, retail competition is better secured by widening the range of goods on sale, thereby increasing consumer choice, than through duplication of suppliers.

11.2. Whilst it is BAA's general policy to let concession contracts by tender this is not done for all of them. If, for example, the Authority identifies and wishes to test a new market opportunity, it may select the most likely concessionaire without seeking other suppliers; depending on the concessionaire the trial period can be as short as six months or as long as five years. At the expiry of the trial period any further concession will be subject to open tender.

11.3. Generally each retail or service outlet is the subject of a separate concession. However, it is BAA's practice to let a single concession combining the duty-free and tax-free outlets at one terminal. In the past these had been offered separately but the most attractive bids had been received for joint operation. BAA told us, moreover, that HM Customs and Excise were unwilling to allow more than one duty-free operator in each terminal. Customs and Excise told us that the relevant statutes did not prohibit such an arrangement but that because of staff shortages they had resisted it. However, if it was shown to be in the public interest to introduce competition where facilities for separate duty-free shops could be provided—as in the case of Terminal 4 at Heathrow—they would endeavour to meet the consequent need for extra supervision.

11.4. At Stansted BAA invited tenders for the duty- and tax-free and tax-paid shops as one concession, because the duty-paid shop was not viable on its own. It is also common practice to invite one tender for all the catering outlets in each terminal. The catering concession at Heathrow Terminal 3 covers seven different outlets. The Authority told us that its existing airport terminals had been designed with a central core of kitchens and support facilities, which does not lend itself to multiple concessionaires.

11.5. At Heathrow Terminal 4 the design of the building will allow two airside catering concessions. Terminal 4 will also have two outlets each combining duty-

and tax-free shops; tenders have been invited for both outlets as a single concession.

11.6. BAA expressed concern at the small number of companies which hold a high proportion of all concessions at its airports, particularly for tax- and duty-free shops and catering (see paragraph 9.4). Efforts have been made to attract a greater range of tenderers for recent contracts and for the concessions currently being offered for Terminal 4 at Heathrow.

BAA pricing policy

11.7. Because any protected market can be abused, the Authority explained that it considers it necessary to control and monitor its concessionaires' prices, particularly for 'necessities'. When considering tenders it also needed to compare various combinations of prices and products. Control of prices varied according to the sensitivity of the activity and its financial importance; the Authority had no single formula. The Authority's intention is that its pricing policy should appear to be reasonable and that concessionaires' customers should obtain good value for money.

Duty-free goods

11.8. The present policy, established by the BAA Board in 1981, is that the prices of standard brands of whisky, gin, vodka and tobacco products in its duty-free shops should show a minimum saving of 37·5 per cent against the average United Kingdom High Street prices. The purpose is to increase sales while protecting the customer from exploitation. The terms of the contracts specify the range of duty-free goods to be stocked (by brands) and the prices to be charged. The income to BAA, specified as a percentage of turnover, is subject to variation by BAA to ensure that the concessionaire's retained margin is unaltered by changes in the costs of his supplies (otherwise BAA could not enforce its policy of a 37·5 per cent saving).

11.9. The selling prices of individual items, whilst subject to the broad percentage saving defined above, are set in the light of United Kingdom High Street prices, and the duty-free prices available at other airports and in-flight. Prices are uniform at all BAA airports irrespective of the concessionaire.

11.10. We received no complaints from concessionaires about the control of duty-free prices. Allders said it thought that control was exercised in a way that, together with the monitoring of the costs of its supplies, ensured that the widest possible range of products was offered at competitive prices.

Tax-free goods

11.11. The prices of tax-free goods are not fixed by the Authority. For all goods other than perfumes and photographic equipment the concession contract stipulates that the prices should not exceed those charged at comparable retail outlets, less VAT. The relevant local retail market is defined in the contract; for the South-East airports it is specified Oxford Street stores. Generally French perfume is sold at 20 per cent, and other perfumes at 25 per cent, less than the local retail price. Prices of photographic goods are determined by the prices shown in a weekly photographic magazine (Camera Weekly), less VAT.

Catering

11.12. Until recently BAA controlled the prices and specification of all items sold by catering concessionaires. This was found to be cumbersome and inflexible. BAA's present policy is to control only the prices of certain 'core' items, ie tea, coffee, pastries, various sandwiches and specified alcoholic and soft drinks. The concessionaire has freedom to introduce other items subject to BAA agreeing price and specification. The Authority retains the right to challenge and reduce the price of any item. As a check on the level of core prices it is now BAA practice to carry out regular price monitoring surveys of the prices charged in comparable outlets.

11.13. THF told us that it welcomed the move to core pricing; it had become easier to adjust the range of products and as a consequence sales per passenger had increased in real terms. Nevertheless it would welcome greater freedom to adjust the range and prices outside the core, as is allowed by other airport authorities.

11.14. The application of price control at the point of sale devolves mostly upon the local airport management rather than BAA Headquarters. There are separate common pricing structures for catering products for the South-East and Scottish airports.

Duty-paid

11.15. Duty-paid goods are sold in Skyshops (confectionery, tobacco, newspapers, books, gifts), and in specialist shops. The new corporate Skyshop identity was introduced by the Authority in 1983. Skyshop concessionaires are normally responsible for providing staff uniforms and point-of-sale material approved by BAA and consistent with a common colour scheme. They are also required to supply goods in plastic bags carrying the Skyshop logo and to stock BAA's 'own brand' merchandise, as well as a specified list of 'brand leaders' which varies between airports.

11.16. John Menzies said that the introduction of the Skyshop concept had removed the benefit which attended the display of the concessionaire's name. It believed that 'staff act more responsibly when directly identified with a company and the company in turn should stand up and be counted in the eyes of the public'.

11.17. BAA said that the purpose of the Skyshop concept was to give these shops an identity which could be used as a platform for promotion. If the concessionaire wanted to use his own name BAA would consider this, seeking to evaluate the strength of the name and its value in commercial terms.

11.18. Contracts require that duty-paid prices should not exceed the manufacturer's recommended or suggested retail price; if these are not available the selling price is not to exceed that normally charged by the concessionaire in his High Street outlets. If this comparison cannot be made the price is to be within the range charged in local off-airport retail outlets. The Authority told us that duty-paid prices are monitored, and comparisons are made through surveys of High Street prices, carried out by consultants.

11.19. Concession contracts do not require any specific number of magazine titles to be stocked. The Periodical Publishers Association complained to us about the limited range of magazines stocked in Skyshops, and in particular at those operated by concessionaires who are not major magazine and newspaper retailers. The Association argued that the range of magazines to be stocked should not be determined by comparing the terms established in the news trade with those available on general merchandise. Its contention was that either BAA should be required to reduce commission from concessionaires on magazine sales, as had been the case in the United States; or publishers should be able to set up competing outlets where the concessionaire does not offer an adequate range. THF told us that in practice BAA's product managers made suggestions about the merchandise range, including titles stocked in the bookshop; generally it accepted them.

Car parking

11.20. At all airports, except Glasgow, BAA sets the prices charged for car parking. At Glasgow, under the terms of a 99-year agreement inherited from the airport's previous owners, NCP sets the prices subject to the Authority's approval. At Gatwick under the terms of its agreement with NCP the Authority has to compensate NCP if charges are not raised in line with inflation. At Heathrow, because of congestion, charges in the central area are set at a relatively high level in order to ration demand; whilst at Stansted the very low charges are designed to encourage use of the airport.

Car rental

11.21. The terms of car rental contracts require that the concessionaires do not charge prices in excess of their national rates (or central London rates for Heathrow contracts). Car rental companies have in practice interpreted the national rate to mean the tariff normally applied for one-way hire. This tariff is common to all United Kingdom airports, both BAA and non-BAA, and where car hire is offered at railway stations. Reductions are offered by the local (non-airport) offices of the major car hire companies for hirings which begin and end at the same office. Avis told us that 72 to 73 per cent of cars hired from airports are returned to the airport of hire.

11.22. We asked BAA if it had considered granting the car hire concessions on the basis of the lowest fares quoted. BAA said it thought there would be difficulty in doing this.

Restrictions on competition

11.23. In the course of our investigation we found several cases of the Authority consciously acting to restrict or prevent competition to its concessionaires. This is sometimes reflected in exclusivity clauses in concession contracts; in other cases BAA actively restricts competition by off-airport suppliers.

100

11.24. Exclusive contracts have been granted generally in respect of duty- and tax-free concessions (which produce most revenue) and banking concessions. In the case of the former the Authority told us its practice was partly determined by the attitude of HM Customs and Excise (see paragraph 11.3), and the possibility that there might otherwise be a rating liability.

11.25. At Gatwick there are two bank concessionaires; elsewhere there is one concessionaire in each airport or terminal. Only for each Heathrow terminal and for Edinburgh are there exclusive contracts. The South-East airport contracts require the concessionaire to encash cheques drawn on other clearing banks without charge. BAA told us that it is trying to extend this requirement to Scotland and intends to include it in future contracts.

11.26. Even where there is no exclusivity clause there are examples of restrictive clauses in contracts preventing direct competition between concessionaires. The 1981 Godfrey Davis Europcar car rental agreement prohibits any cut-price offers, special promotional offers, discounts or inducements related to the concessionaire's airport business without the prior written consent of the Authority.[1] (Godfrey Davis Europcar had not sought to introduce any such offers.) Under the April 1985 agreement for the Heathrow Terminal 1 giftshop only the approved list of goods may be sold, and the concessionaire is prohibited, without prior written approval, from offering a Retail Export Scheme where goods are sold exclusive of VAT or VAT can be refunded. More generally, the Authority, even in non-exclusive agreements, stipulates the list of goods which may be sold.

11.27. BAA considers that it has an obligation to protect concessionaires against direct competition from off-airport suppliers; the concessionaires have paid for the right to trade on the airport and their activities there are largely regulated; off-airport operators could, if they wished, tender for the concession. Two examples of the Authority preventing such competition to duty- and tax-free concessionaires were brought to our notice by Britannia Airlines and British Caledonian. Both had tried to advertise their on-plane duty-free prices at their check-in desks, but BAA stopped them. The Authority told us that its policy was to maximise its income from duty-free concessions, and it objected to the airlines trying to deflect passengers from visiting the shops. Moreover, such advertising was prohibited by the licences for check-in desks and this was known to the airlines when the licences were granted.

11.28. Another case of restriction of competition by off-airport suppliers was brought to our notice by Town and Country Car Rentals which offers services from an off-airport site near the Heathrow perimeter, and from hotels near Gatwick, Glasgow, Edinburgh and Prestwick. The company believed it met a demand for lower cost rental; it would be unable to do so if it had to pay a significant percentage of its revenue to BAA for a concession, and it had therefore not tendered for one. About half of its business was pre-booked, and pre-paid, with the remainder coming from its advertisements in magazines and elsewhere.

---

[1]BAA told us that a substantial proportion of bookings are made at a discount, for example as part of a fly-drive arrangement.

101

11.29. Town and Country encountered three difficulties in competing with on-airport concessionaires. The first arose out of inadequate signposting in the terminals to the off-airport operators' pick-up points. Town and Country said that pre-booked clients frequently could not find this point, even though they had been given instructions before their flight; consequently they often then booked with a concessionaire. The company had suggested to BAA that it be allowed to provide 'meet and greet' staff who would help the traveller to the pick-up point and fill in the rental agreement. It was able to operate in this way at Manchester and Birmingham airports. Recognising that it might obtain additional business by casual customers approaching such staff, Town and Country offered to pay BAA a percentage on any extra business it obtained in this way, but the Authority refused.[1] The Authority told us it had decided to improve the signs to pick-up points for off-airport car hire operators at Heathrow.

11.30. Secondly, Town and Country had attemped to advertise through More O'Ferrall (the BAA concessionaire for poster advertising space) at Heathrow, and on the display cubes at Gatwick, and had been turned down because, it understood, it was a car rental operation. BAA told us it was its policy not to allow any company in competition with its concessionaires to advertise at airports.

11.31. The final difficulty concerned the provision sought by the company of a box into which returning passengers could deposit car keys after leaving a car in the car park. BAA had not agreed to provide this facility.

The tendering process—general procedure

11.32. The process by which concessions are let is clearly set out. The instructions to BAA staff detail comprehensively what is expected both of airport and of Head Office staff, and we found that they were being followed. Minor differences between airports were justified by local conditions. The evaluation of tenders was thorough and the evaluation report provided comprehensive detail for the tender panel to make its judgment.

The tendering process—case studies

11.33. We examined the granting of two recent concessions, for public catering at Glasgow and for the duty-free, tax-free, and duty-paid shops at Stansted, in order to see to what extent competition operates at the tendering stage.

Glasgow airport public catering

11.34. Tenders for the concession for public catering were invited in January 1985 for a five-year contract; prior to this 14 companies were invited for interviews. Two companies withdrew before the interview and a further four were not invited to tender after being interviewed.

11.35. The tender documents set out information on the general background of the airport, the catering facilities available and an outline of the contract.

---

[1] BAA told us that pre-booked car rentals accounted for between 59 per cent and 95 per cent of hirings at its various airports.

Detailed monthly passenger statistics for the past five years were provided, and BAA forecasts of the numbers of domestic and international passengers for each of the next five years. Passenger statistics showing the peak and trough flows on a monthly and hourly basis were given, together with aircraft movements for the latest year showing the summer and winter schedule by time of flight and aircraft type. The tender offer made it clear that there were peaks in demand for catering. BAA views on future developments of public catering were set out, and the need for new buffet services for the BMA and British Airways departure lounges was stressed. BAA stated that none of the information supplied was part of the contract.

11.36. The tenderers were required to bid a percentage of turnover to be paid to BAA for each of seven categories of food, drink, confectionery and tobacco goods. The initial tender offer contained details of monthly sales (1982 to 1984) for four broad areas. Information on sales of the seven categories was subsequently supplied in reponse to requests from prospective tenderers.

11.37. The tender offer and the agreement set out the opening hours of the facilities, and the seating capacity available. A detailed product specification was given which, for example, stipulated the content of various types of sandwich. The current price schedule was supplied and BAA's policy of controlling core prices explained, as was its right to set all prices if it so desired. The tenderer was also required to provide details of staffing levels for each catering facility and sales forecasts for six years for each of the seven categories.

Tender evaluation

11.38. Tenders were evaluated on financial and non-financial grounds. For the financial evaluation BAA prepared its own sales forecast for each product category and calculated the income from each tenderer. The majority of the tenderers had forecast higher sales levels.

11.39. The non-financial evaluation was carried out by the catering Product Manager. At that stage he did not know the tenderers' financial bids. The evaluation comprised a check list for each tenderer's products, staffing, marketing, staff training, experience, and management. A 'mark out of ten' was given for each item in the check list, the mark being based on the tender proposal, and BAA's knowledge of the tenderer's operations elsewhere. Particular attention was paid to the ability to meet peak demands, and the appropriateness to the market of the pricing and products offered.

11.40. The successful tenderer was recommended by both the financial and non-financial evaluations.

Stansted airport — duty-free, tax-free and duty-paid concession

11.41. In 1978 THF won a five-year concession, which was later extended for three years with an agreed reduction in the percentage payable to BAA. In 1984 THF sought a reduction of [*] percentage points in the terms because of a change in the passenger mix, but BAA refused to concede so nine months' notice of termination was agreed between the parties.

* Figure omitted. See note on page iv.

11.42. A new five-year exclusive contract was advertised in July 1984; of those who responded only THF and Allders were regarded as suitable, and were invited to tender. Similar background information was given as for the Glasgow catering concession. The operating hours of the duty-paid shop were specified, and it was a condition of the contract that the duty- and tax-free, and airside duty-paid shops be open for all departing flights. The products, and their prices for duty-free sale, were specified in a schedule to the contract and BAA's pricing policy was set out. The appointed concessionaire was required to submit a full list of price proposals two months prior to the start of the contract. BAA reserved the right to instruct the concessionaire to reduce prices, and could also require it to submit a comparison of its prices with London High Street stores.

11.43. BAA supplied sales data disaggregated to 26 product groups. The tenderer was required to provide separate percentage bids for 56 product groups, together with a marketing plan for the first year. Subsequent annual plans were to be provided. The marketing plan had to include:

(a) sales forecasts for each of the main product groups;

(b) layout plans for the merchandise;

(c) staffing levels for mid-week and weekends for spring/summer and autumn/winter, including hourly coverage by staff grade;

(d) details of staff training programme;

(e) point of sale and packaging proposals; and

(f) a full schedule of weekly promotions of liquor, tobacco products etc.

It was also a requirement that the concessionaire carry out market research, to be made available to BAA.

Tender evaluation

11.44. On the financial evaluation, using BAA's own sales forecasts for each product group, THF outbid Allders. The non-financial evaluation concluded that there was little to choose between them, although Allders had an advantage in respect of the tax-free sales within the overall duty- and tax-free sector. BAA felt that this advantage was not sufficient to outweigh the overall financial advantages of the THF tender, and awarded the contract accordingly.

11.45. In the new contract THF has obtained a reduction of approximately [*] percentage points compared with its earlier contract.

Licence arrangements for services to airlines

Handling at Heathrow

11.46. Prior to the early 1970s any airline operating at Heathrow could, subject to facilities being available, provide for itself the full range of ground handling services (see paragraph 4.6). The eight airlines which did so were known as 'self-handlers'; other airlines bought some or all of these services from the self-handlers, or from third party suppliers.

---

* Figure omitted. See note on page iv.

11.47. BAA told us that because of the problems caused by the airside proliferation of vehicles and equipment and the shortage of facilities within terminals, a freeze was placed in 1978 on any extension to self-handling. This freeze was accepted by the Airline Operators Committee. Since then further rights to operate any of these services have been controlled by the issue of licences to third parties, and by the terms of rental agreements with airlines. Tables 11.1 to 11.3 show the provision of the principal services to airlines at each of the three terminals at Heathrow. BAA restricts the provision of services to others by the self-handlers to the terminals in which they operate, except for British Airways which operates out of Terminals 1 and 3 but provides handling services in Terminal 2 as well (see footnote to paragraph 4.7).

TABLE 11.1 **Provision of airline services at Heathrow Terminal 1**

	Self-handlers		Non-self-handlers
Service	Aer Lingus	BA	6 other airlines
Baggage handling	Self	Self	3 Aer Lingus, 3 BA
Aircraft loading	Self	Self	3 Aer Lingus, 3 BA
Aircraft cleaning	Self/Skyliner	Self	2 BA, 1 Skyliner, 1 Aer Lingus, 1 Aer Lingus/THF
Aircraft catering	Marriott	Self	2 THF, 1 SAS, 3 non-catering
Crew transportation	Self/Martons	Self	1 Aer Lingus, 1 BA, 2 British Midland, 2 without transportation
Check-in	Self	Self	1 Aer Lingus, 2 British Midland, 3 BA

Source: BAA.

TABLE 11.2 **Provision of airline services at Heathrow Terminal 2**

	Self-handlers		Non-self-handlers
Service	KLM	Air France	26 other airlines
Baggage handling	Self	Self	21 BA, 1 KLM, 4 Air France
Aircraft handling	Self	Self	20 BA, 1 self, 1 KLM, 4 Air France
Aircraft cleaning	THF	Skyliner	16 BA, 6 Skyliner, 2 THF, 1 Air France, 1 Swift
Aircraft catering	THF	THF	2 BA, 1 self, 4 Marriott, 11 THF, 5 SAS, 2 Dobbs, 1 N/A
Crew transportation	Self	Martons	9 BA, 1 KLM, 7 Martons, 1 Gold Eagle, 8 N/A
Check-in	Self	Self	17 BA, 1 KLM, 4 Air France, 1 Lufthansa, 3 self

Source: BAA.

Note: British Airways does not operate out of Terminal 2, but handles other carriers.

11.48. When the freeze was introduced in 1978 the Authority considered that the ideal solution to the problems at Heathrow would be the introduction of one agent who would undertake the obligation to provide a service at any terminal on demand. An earlier attempt, unconnected with the freeze, had been made to

Table 11.3 **Provision of airline services at Heathrow Terminal 3**

Service	BA	Air Canada	Air India	Pan Am	TWA	28 other airlines
			Self-handlers			*Non-self-handlers*
Baggage	Self	Self	Self	Self	Self	11 BA, 9 Aer Lingus, 5 Air Canada, 3 Pan Am
Aircraft loading	Self	Self	Self	Self	Self	11 BA, 9 Aer Lingus, 5 Air Canada, 3 Pan Am
Aircraft cleaning	Self	Self	Marriott	Self	THF	9 BA, 13 THF, 1 BA/THF, 4 Air Canada, 1 Skyliner
Aircraft catering	Self	Self	SAS	THF	Marriott	2 BA, 6 Dobbs, 12 THF, 1 self, 3 Marriott, 3 SAS, 1 International Catering
Crew transportation	Self	Martons	Martons/ Angel	Capital Coaches	Martons	8 BA, 7 Martons, 7 Capital Coaches, 3 Angel, 2 self, 1 airline without
Check-in	Self	Self	Self	Self	Self	6 BA, 4 self/BA, 10 self, 4 Air Canada, 1 self/Air Canada, 1 Pan Am, 2 self/Pan Am

Source: BAA.

introduce such an agent in 1969 but the attempt failed because of widespread industrial action. In 1982 in agreement with the Airline Operators Committee the Authority made another attempt on a different basis. The invitation to tender for the position of 'nominated handler' was limited to the eight self-handlers with 'grandfather' rights. Only British Airways and Aer Lingus expressed interest, and Aer Lingus was awarded the contract although a formal agreement for five years was not signed until January 1984.

11.49. The handling arrangements covered by the Aer Lingus agreement are: passenger handling (check-in etc), baggage handling, aircraft handling, aircraft cleaning, aircraft catering, cargo handling, aircraft servicing and maintenance, and crew transportation. Aer Lingus is obliged to provide a service to any other airline at any terminal on request (unlike the other self-handlers, who have rights but no obligations) and BAA will provide necessary facilities. The agreement gives the Authority the right to ask Aer Lingus to justify its charges. BAA will receive a licence fee of [*] per cent of turnover under any new contracts gained by Aer Lingus after January 1984. BAA told us that Aer Lingus had so far not gained any such contracts. It can be seen from Tables 11.1 to 11.3 that Aer Lingus holds contracts in Terminal 1 for baggage handling, aircraft loading, cleaning, crew transportation and check-in and in Terminal 3 for baggage handling.

11.50. Under the agreement BAA will use its best endeavours to ensure that the range of handling services carried out by any other airline is not increased; airlines at present providing services to other airlines may continue to do so providing that they limit these to their own terminals; the Authority will not enter into a similar agreement with any other airline or company.

* Figure omitted. See note on page iv.

11.51. British Midland Airways (BMA) complained to us that although it was the second largest carrier at Heathrow in terms of ATMs the Authority had refused to allow it to handle its own traffic in Terminal 1. In 1984 it had almost two and a half times as many ATMs as Aer Lingus and, with the exception of British Airways, nearly twice as many as any other airline operating from Terminal 1. To provide its handling services it had to choose between Aer Lingus and British Airways, the latter being its competitor on important domestic routes. Apart from reluctance to use a competitor, British Airways' quoted charges for handling services were considerably in excess of those proposed by Aer Lingus. BMA has no complaint about the quality of service provided by Aer Lingus, but is seriously concerned about the level of charges. From its own experience of handling at Birmingham it thinks that it could have provided the services itself at only just over half the amount paid to Aer Lingus. It believes that this difference is a substantial element in its competitiveness, and it would be able to pass on the benefits of lower handling charges to its customers.

11.52. The Authority investigated the Aer Lingus charges, and told BMA that it thought them reasonable. However, BMA believes that for historical reasons Aer Lingus has extremely high labour costs, and that it passes them on in its charges.

11.53. BAA told us that there was insufficient accommodation to permit BMA to self-handle. Moreover, it would be a significant departure from the policy to freeze handling rights and could lead to other airlines wanting similar facilities. Foreign airlines were often backed by diplomatic pressure at a high level. The Authority had decided to review its ground handling policy one year after Terminal 4 was opened; subject to this review, which would include consideration of radical changes, airlines with handling rights moving to Terminal 1 would retain them.

11.54. BMA does not believe these reasons to be valid. It says there is sufficient accommodation for a ramp handling unit at Terminal 1, and if it took over the equipment used by Aer Lingus to handle BMA's traffic there would be no net increase. As regards changes which might result from the opening of Terminal 4, BMA says the Authority has since 1978 advanced successive reasons for not allowing it to self-handle. BMA suggests that no other airline at Heathrow has the volume of traffic which would make it anxious to self-handle, and in any event, the Authority could have a different policy for domestic services at Terminal 1.

11.55. The Authority told us that among the eight airlines who have ground handling rights there was a certain amount of unused capacity at particular times of day, although no study had been carried out to establish precisely what spare capacity existed in terms of staff and equipment. All the equipment used by handling airlines was subject to airside passes and licences. BAA told us that it had never refused any application for these, although if it observed any equipment which had not been used for two or three weeks the matter would be taken up with the owner. BAA had considered charging a rent for apron parking areas to reduce the airside proliferation of equipment but felt that the existence of 'grandfather' rights would make this difficult. The situation would be reviewed after the opening of Terminal 4.

Handling at Gatwick

11.56. BAA told us that it had been able to establish a system of handling rights at Gatwick, in the early development of the airport, which averted many of the problems met at Heathrow, and provided for competition. The number of handling agents is limited to three: British Airways, British Caledonian, and Gatwick Handling (GH).

11.57. GH was formed as a joint venture between Dan-Air and Laker; the Laker share was subsequently sold in equal proportions to Northwest Orient Airlines, and Delta Airlines (both American companies). The original agreement with GH was for ten years; the current agreement is subject to termination by either party on 12 months' notice. BAA incorporated a clause in this agreement to ensure that serious consideration would be given to any airline operating on a substantial basis at Gatwick which might wish to purchase an interest in the equity of GH. BAA has a right under the agreement to approve the prices charged by GH, subject to GH not being placed at a competitive disadvantage.

11.58. GH pays a percentage of turnover as a licence fee, whereas British Airways and British Caledonian pay rent for their check-in desks, baggage facilities and cargo sheds. The Authority does not attempt to adjust these different arrangements so as to produce comparable charges for similar levels of activity.

11.59. Britannia Airways told us that BAA's refusal to extend handling rights at Gatwick 'gives unfair advantages—political, commercial and operational' to its major competitors, British Airways, British Caledonian and Dan-Air. Britannia said that at airports where there is a handling agency which is not an airline costs tend to be lower, including handling charges made by airlines. At the time of the Laker collapse the Receiver had invited bids for the whole or part of the Laker holding in GH. Britannia made the best offer and would have been acceptable to BAA. Dan-Air was not prepared, however, to agree to Britannia becoming an equal partner and the latter would not accept less.

11.60. The Authority said that some of the airlines which do not self-handle had wanted to carry out their own check-in at Gatwick but this had been refused because of space constraints in the terminal. BAA's current view is that the policy to have only three handling agents will continue at Gatwick for both the existing terminal and the new North Terminal. BAA's aim was to provide a choice of at least two handlers in the new terminal.

Handling at Glasgow

11.61. BAA provides all the freight handling, baggage handling, and aircraft handling services at Glasgow with no airline having self-handling rights. Five airlines provide their own check-in facilities and a rent is charged for the desk and associated services. Check-in services are provided to over 20 other airlines by Servisair, which has a 12-year agreement with BAA under which it pays a desk rental and a percentage on turnover. The agreement is non-exclusive and provides for no control over Servisair's prices.

In-flight catering at Heathrow

11.62. At Heathrow in-flight catering may be provided by any of the self-handlers, and also by El-Al. BAA receives no fee for catering carried out by any of them, except for new contracts with Aer Lingus. Four off-airport caterers are also licensed for three years: Dobbs, Marriott, SAS and International Catering. They pay a fee of 6 per cent of turnover on all sales to airlines. THF provides in-flight catering from accommodation sited on the airport and has a leasehold agreement under which it pays a rent and a percentage of turnover.

11.63. The licences of the four off-airport in-flight caterers contain restrictions on the licensee. The services to be provided are specified in the licence, and any change in the specifications requires the consent of BAA. The Authority also requires details of existing and new contracts between the licensee and airlines. The provision of airside licences is something BAA seeks to limit. It will only consider new licences for catering after receiving representations from the individual airlines or the AOCs. Licences are not offered for tender but follow from such nominations. BAA told us that the specification of services is not used in practice as a restriction on competition, but merely as part of the knowledge BAA requires for the efficient operation of the airport.

In-flight catering at Gatwick and Glasgow

11.64. At Gatwick in-flight catering is provided by four off-airport caterers, who pay BAA a licence fee of 6 per cent of turnover. BAA has not so far refused any requests by the AOC to increase the number of caterers. Similar restrictions to those at Heathrow operate in the licences.

11.65. At Glasgow the in-flight caterers are Trusthouse Forte and Air Cuisine. Both have kitchens on the airport, have 50- and 21-year leases respectively, and in addition to the rental for land pay a percentage of turnover. After Air Cuisine began operations at Glasgow in 1982 the cost to airlines of in-flight catering services fell. An approach had been received from a further caterer for a licence to trade but this had been refused. The airlines have not approached BAA for further licensees. BAA told us that the licences contain a requirement for the operators to inform it of the airlines which they serve, but this does not imply that it is necessary to obtain BAA's consent to these arrangements.

Conclusions

11.66. The extent of competition at point of sale is limited by the lack of space within airport terminals.[1] Nevertheless even where competition would be possible, either directly or through promotional activities, BAA effectively restricts or prevents it. It believes that it has an obligation to offer a considerable

---

[1]The Chairman of the Authority said, however, that he hoped the new Heathrow Terminal 4 would include enough space to introduce competition in catering for the first time. When our report was nearly complete BAA told us that all the catering outlets in Terminal 4 had nevertheless been let to a single concessionaire, who does not hold a catering concession at any other BAA airport.

3162890

H

degree of protection to concessionaires who, through competitive tendering, have won the right to trade on its airports.

11.67. The Authority believes that consumer choice is better secured through variety of products for sale than through duplication of suppliers and tries to ensure that the consumer obtains value for money by fixing the prices to be charged directly, or by reference to prices charged outside the airport. We do not believe that these procedures are fully effective in serving the interests of consumers. We therefore recommend a number of small, but not insignificant, ways in which competition at airports can be increased for the benefit of users.

11.68. The evaluation of tenders is thorough, but it is a matter of some concern that the concessions at BAA airports are concentrated among relatively few companies. Such concentration reduces the likelihood of the introduction of different trading methods and limits the scope for BAA to compare different concessionaires. It has tried to attract a greater range of tenderers for the concessions being offered for Terminal 4, and we recommend that this practice is applied wherever possible.

11.69. Our case studies of the tendering procedures revealed two instances where BAA had not provided a full sales breakdown of the products for which it required percentage bids although in one case these were subsequently given in response to a request. We do not base any general criticism of the tendering procedure on these instances. The Authority should seek to ensure that full information is provided at the outset; and that the time allowed for the preparation of tenders is adequate not only for existing concessionaires but also for new tenderers.

11.70. Skyshop concessionaires should be allowed to trade under their own names. This would provide both them and their staffs with an incentive to maintain their public image and enable the public to be aware from whom they were buying. The incorporation of the concessionaire's name alongside the Skyshop logo would not detract from BAA's promotional activity.

11.71. The terms of car rental concessions allow the car rental companies to charge national one-way rates although most customers at airports are seeking return hire; we think this is wrong. BAA told us that it will review these terms in the light of our finding, and we recommend that appropriate changes are introduced as soon as practicable. BAA should facilitate further competition in car rentals and allow off-airport car rental operators to advertise at BAA airports without discrimination. The Authority should also provide adequate signposting and coach pick-up facilities for off-airport operators.

11.72. BAA told us that it would not allow publicity at its airports for competitors to any of its concessionaires. We consider this to be an unfair restriction on competition and recommend that this discrimination should cease.

11.73. We recognise the difficulties BAA has in rationalising ground handling at Heathrow because of the existence of the 'grandfather' rights of the self-handling airlines, which prevent the most efficient use of handling resources.

11.74. BMA brought to our attention the particular situation at Heathrow Terminal 1, where the choice of ground handlers is limited to Aer Lingus and British Airways. Since a number of the airlines using Terminal 1 are in competition with British Airways this effectively means that they have no choice. BMA is the second largest carrier in terms of ATMs, significantly larger than many of those airlines with self-handling rights. It told us it could achieve significant savings if granted self-handling rights.

11.75. We believe the degree of choice available to airlines without self-handling rights is unsatisfactory. We recommend that the Authority should arrange that in each Heathrow terminal an airline without self-handling rights has a choice of at least two handlers, neither of which is an airline with which it is in competition. In making these arrangements BAA should not limit its consideration to airlines with existing self-handling rights, and should take account of the charges made to airlines and the cost savings achievable.

11.76. We recommend that on expiry of the Aer Lingus contract the position of nominated handler should be open to tender from any airline using Heathrow (whether or not that airline currently has handling rights), and to any outside handling agency.

11.77. The existing self-handlers should be free to undertake business in any terminal, particularly where this would improve the utilisation of equipment. To this end we recommend that BAA surveys with the Airline Operators Committee the utilisation of all handling equipment and staff at Heathrow and the charges made.

11.78. The opening of the North Terminal at Gatwick will provide BAA with an opportunity to invite tenders from other would-be handlers in addition to those airlines with existing handling rights. We recommend that BAA does this, and establishes the degree of choice we have prescribed in paragraph 11.75.

11.79. Our terms of reference require us to consider what scope there is for competition at the point of sale. Although we have made suggestions which should give some impetus to competitive pressure, the scope for competition *in* this market is very limited. The benefits of effective competition may under certain circumstances be achieved via the alternative route of effective competition *for* the market. In the case of BAA, however, this form of competition has not been fully effective either. The problem is partly due (see paragraph 11.68) to the limited number of companies that tender for a concession and the inherent advantages that the incumbent concessionaire has over potential entrants. It is also due, however, to the fact that the form of BAA concessions, and the basis upon which tenders are judged, benefits the Authority rather than the consumer. This is most noticeable in the case of duty- and tax-free goods where the mark-up on costs is high, as is BAA's proportion of the sales revenue (see Table 9.4). This approach is consistent with the Authority's policy ' to maximise profit in its commercial affairs ' but may not be ' consistent ... with its obligations as a public enterprise ' (see paragraph 4.14). An alternative approach might be to let concession contracts on a different basis, for example with a fixed rental and prescribed standards of service, judging between tenders on the lowest prices proposed to be charged to customers.

CHAPTER 12

Manpower efficiency and industrial relations

Staff numbers, productivity and manpower planning

12.1. The Authority's total workforce is just under 7,000; of these 292 were engaged on commercial activities (as defined in our terms of reference) on 28 March 1985. A breakdown of these by location and broad functional category is shown in Table 12.1. Staff employed by concessionaires, licensees and tenants are outside our terms of reference.

TABLE 12.1 **BAA staff engaged on commercial activities*** (including secretarial staff)

Location	Fully engaged	Part engaged	Total
Head Office			
—Trading†	56	—	56
—Property	12	—	12
—Others	—	7	7
Heathrow			
—Commercial†	24	36	60‡
—Property	30	5	35
—Car parks	18	2	20
Gatwick			
—Commercial‡	7	17	24
—Property	10	—	10
—Car parks	6	—	6
Stansted	1	8	9
Scottish Airports HQ	4	5	9
Glasgow	3	5	8
Edinburgh	—	11	11
Prestwick	3	12	15
Aberdeen	2	8	10
Total	176	116	292

Source: BAA.

*As defined in our terms of reference.

†As defined in paragraph 5.37.

‡Includes the property function in terminals where property and commercial functions are integrated.

12.2. About 40 per cent of the staff shown in the table are also engaged on other activities. BAA told us that for this reason it considered it impracticable to establish the exact number of staff hours spent on commercial activities (as defined in our terms of reference), particularly as the percentage of time many of them spent on other activities varied according to operational requirements: it was thus impracticable to establish meaningful productivity measures for commercial activities alone.

12.3. Two performance targets agreed with the Department of Transport for 1983–84 to 1985–86 are to reduce costs (at constant prices) per terminal passenger and to increase the number of terminal passengers per payroll hour. In each case the target is to improve by 0·5 per cent per annum plus two-fifths of the passenger growth over the three-year period. Table 12.2 shows actual and projected achievements against these performance aims.

TABLE 12.2. **Costs per passenger and passengers per payroll hour, 1982–83 to 1985–86**

		Costs per passenger* £	Passengers per payroll hour
1982–83	(Base year)	4·87	2·60
1983–84	Target	4·73	2·68
1983–84	Actual	4·63	2·80
1984–85	Target	4·49	2·81
1984–85	Actual	4·31	3·12
1985–86	Target	4·36	2·86
1985–86	Projected	4·30	2·98

Source: BAA.

*At constant March 1985 prices.

12.4. The Corporate Plan includes a manpower plan with projections for five years, which represent assessments by line management of staffing needs based on traffic forecasts, likely changes in working practices and other developments. These estimates are also contained in each Airport Business Plan introduced in 1983 and compiled annually.

12.5. The current manpower forecast reflects expected increases as a result of the development of the new Heathrow Terminal 4 and Gatwick North Terminal, and the need seen by BAA to expand its Management Services function. Between 1985–86 and 1989–90 total staff numbers are forecast to grow by 6·8 per cent compared with a forecast traffic growth of 18 per cent. Details of these forecasts are shown in Appendix 12.1.

12.6. The Authority has a management development scheme for all non-industrial staff, the key elements of which are open performance appraisal incorporating personal targets, regular career counselling and succession planning.

12.7. The system of setting targets for individual managers was first introduced for the year 1983–84, and is seen as a management tool and a motivation for managers arising naturally from the preparation of the Business Plan. Wherever possible targets are set in financial terms relating to the BAA costs/revenues for which the manager is responsible. Other targets are set in terms of job content, eg 'complete all ... by end of the year'. Targets generally extend down to middle management for the purposes of the Business Plan but may be used at lower levels as part of the general system of personnel appraisal. Each target will be agreed between the individual concerned and the responsible higher level of management, and not normally made known to others.

Recruitment

12.8. When the filling of a vacancy has been approved by the appropriate senior officer details will normally be included on internal vacancy notices, unless it is filled by the transfer of an individual who has been identified as suitable for the job through BAA's management development process. If the necessary expertise may not exist within BAA the vacancy is also advertised externally. Of the 56 staff currently employed in BAA's Trading Department, ten have been recruited from outside. The Authority told us that it has no difficulty in recruiting staff of the right calibre in this area.

Grading, salary structures and productivity scheme

12.9. All jobs below senior management within BAA are subject to centralised job evaluation schemes administered jointly with the trade unions. Current pay scales for non-industrial staff up to Band 1 are shown in Appendix 12.2. BAA has a total of 53 senior management staff who are on a separate unpublished salary structure above Band 1.

12.10. With effect from August 1977 the Authority agreed with its trade unions the introduction of a productivity scheme which allowed for payments of up to 10 per cent of salary based on the ratio of added value to employee costs. In the past three years payments have averaged between 9 and 10 per cent of basic pay.

Training

12.11. BAA's Central Training Branch has responsibility for the formation of policy for the development, education and training of staff. It also runs training courses open to candidates from the whole organisation. Over the five years to 1984–85 BAA has increased its total spending on training by 113 per cent, but expenditure on training trading and commercial staff has increased by over 130 per cent in the three years to 1984–85. An innovation in 1980 was the 'Managing for Productivity' programme. BAA said this succeeded in 'broadening [its] managers' understanding of human resource management and introducing ... a way of learning which not only makes line managers responsible for training but also involves them as trainers'. A number of further programmes have been developed to build on this base.

12.12. Another innovation, aimed at improving the overall effectiveness of BAA's service, has been the ' Please the Passenger ' campaign. This is a video-based training programme, incorporating specially prepared publicity material, and until recently included the ' In search of gold ' competition which offered a Mini Metro to the member of staff putting forward the best suggestion for improving standards of service to passengers.

Collective bargaining arrangements

12.13. Under the Airports Authority Act 1975, BAA has a duty to consult with appropriate trade unions and to establish and maintain machinery for 'the settlement by negotiation of terms and conditions of employment of persons employed by the BAA'. For this purpose the Authority recognises ten trade unions which represent industrial and non-industrial staff. BAA does not have trade union membership agreements but actively encourages staff to join an appropriate trade union. The present level of union membership in BAA is approximately 80 per cent.

12.14. BAA's machinery for negotiation and consultation is well established and operates at all levels throughout the organisation. It is shown in Appendix 12.3. In addition to the central committees and sub-committees there is a Scottish Airports Joint Committee and local bodies operating at each airport. The organisation for Heathrow is shown in Appendix 12.4.

12.15. All unions are represented on the central joint bodies. The Central Joint Council, chaired by BAA's Chairman, is a consultative committee. It meets at least once a year and discusses the Authority's Annual Report and Accounts. The Joint Negotiating and Consultative Committee, chaired by the Managing Director, is the final stage in the central negotiating machinery and in the grievance procedure. It meets at least twice a year.

12.16. Below this tier is the Joint Standing Committee which is essentially the 'working' level of the central machinery. Chaired by the Personnel Director it meets at least six times a year, and has constitutional authority to set up working parties to consider specific subjects in detail. Additionally it ratifies decisions of its four sub-committees. The Central Joint Council held two meetings during 1984–85 and there were 23 joint meetings of the other central negotiating and consultative committees.

12.17. The secretaries of the trade union sides of the committees for Heathrow, Gatwick and Scottish airports are engaged full-time on trade union duties. So also is the full-time trades union secretary to the central joint bodies, who is based at BAA's Head Office and is responsible for co-ordinating the trade union side's activities at central level.

12.18. Since the establishment of the joint machinery in 1966 BAA has, in agreement with the unions, extended lay representation as the Authority has developed its commitment to participation and employee involvement. The main effect of changes introduced in 1983 has been to increase the involvement of lay representatives in the decision-making process; in particular by the setting up of small, subject-orientated, joint working parties, which report back to the main committees.

Other communications

12.19. In addition to the formal and informal system for joint consultation, direct communication between managers and staff is emphasised in management training and increasing use is being made of video tapes for this purpose. Staff notices are distributed on a wide range of subjects, as are news releases and a house journal.

Industrial relations

12.20. There has been no industrial dispute involving BAA staff engaged on commercial activities. Staff in the Trading Department have co-operated in some fairly radical changes involving the introduction of new technology and improved working practices.

Conclusions

12.21. Although it has not been possible to apportion accurately the man-hours spent on commercial activities we have seen no evidence of over- or under-staffing. We are satisfied that the downward pressure on staffing numbers stemming from performance targets has been effective. Our conclusion, necessarily based on subjective judgment, is that there is a high level of expertise and effectiveness among BAA's staff responsible for its commercial activities.

12.22. Recognising that insufficient emphasis had been given to its commercial activities BAA has in the last three years devoted considerable resources to training the trading and commercial staff involved. We hope that the Authority will be able to carry out an objective assessment of the effects of this training.

12.23. BAA has a satisfactory system through which its industrial relations are conducted and in our examination of its commercial activities we have been aware of a feeling of common purpose among staff at all levels.

CHAPTER 13

Quality of service

Introduction

13.1. From paragraph 2.1 it can be seen that our reference is under section 11(1)(*b*) as well as section 11(1)(*a*) of the Competition Act 1980. It requires us to investigate and report on whether BAA in its commercial activities could 'improve its efficiency or reduce its costs *or improve the service provided*' (emphasis added), with particular reference *inter alia* to 'the monitoring and control by the Authority of the standard of services provided to passengers by concessionaires'.

13.2. In paragraph 5.9 we noted the ten 'essential policies' which support BAA's main objective. The 'essential policy' most relevant to quality of service is:

> To improve, as far as its powers permit, the range and quality not only of services offered to its customers, but also those provided by other organisations and to have regard to the best practice of other airport authorities in the United Kingdom and abroad.

Other relevant policies are those which refer to meeting 'the needs of airport users for the provision of goods and services' and upholding 'a high standard of design in every aspect which is cost-effective and visually and functionally appropriate'.

13.3. Whether commercial service and commercial profit are complementary, or whether they have to be 'traded off' against each other, is important to our consideration of quality of service. BAA accepts that when allocating space amongst its main trading product areas—duty-free, tax-free, arrivals (for example, car rental, hotel booking, banking), duty-paid, catering and 'new products', it cannot be influenced exclusively by forecast revenue per square foot. Catering facilities and availability of 'distress purchases' in duty-paid shops are examples of required passenger services which do not necessarily produce the maximum profit. In the Trading Department's Marketing Plan Summary 1985 a distinction is made between passenger needs which it is 'necessary' and which it is 'profitable' to meet.

13.4. In its day-to-day activities BAA relies on several ways of monitoring the quality of service. BAA told us that turnover was 'in an overall sense a medium-to long-term reflection of good service'.

Methods of controlling and monitoring service

Service standards

13.5. In the planning of passenger terminals, 'service standards' are specified, mostly for non-commercial aspects of airport/terminal operation. These are concerned with the safety and convenience of passengers and with the speed with

117

which they can pass through the terminal. Service standards cover, for example, queueing time in immigration, baggage service times and space in waiting areas. A list of those used in planning is at Appendix 13.1.

13.6. Whereas service standards at present cover mostly non-commercial aspects of service, other means of monitoring and control cover both commercial and non-commercial matters.

Comment cards

13.7. Comment cards are available to passengers at all terminals. BAA analyses complaints, compliments and other comments. At each airport statistical summaries of comments are passed to the Passenger Services sub-Committee of the Airport Consultative Committee at monthly intervals, and a report on these is included in the Monthly Management Report to the BAA Board.

Passenger service improvement objectives

13.8. BAA is experimenting with ' passenger service improvement objectives '. Ten broad BAA targets agreed by the Board with the Managing Director in 1983 included two internal targets specific to passenger service, one concerning the level of complaints and the other the availability of 'passenger-sensitive' equipment (lifts, escalators, travellators, etc).

13.9. As at December 1984 the complaint-level target was that adverse card comments and other written complaints should not exceed 15 per 100,000 passengers. It had been the intention for some time, however, to supplement the comment card system with a more comprehensive system derived from the passenger opinion surveys (paragraph 13.11). From the categories covered by the opinion surveys, BAA picked three for which objectives would be set, trolley service (departures only), landside catering, and BAA uniformed staff (security, information, porters).

13.10. In December 1984 the Board decided that the objective for landside catering should be: ' In 1985–86 at least 78 per cent of departing passengers using landside catering facilities should express satisfaction.' (The 'current performance' was 75·7 per cent of passengers surveyed.)

Passenger opinion surveys

13.11. BAA's continuous research programme into passenger opinions began in the summer of 1983. Previously, BAA attitudinal surveys had been conducted only intermittently and had concentrated on the summer traffic peaks. They were less easily linked with target-setting in the area of service standards.

13.12. BAA's stated objective for its passenger opinion surveys is 'to establish, in a reasonably scientific manner, the views of passengers at the BAA's airports about various aspects of the services provided at each airport '.

13.13. In the first year of the continuous research a total of some 20,000 departing passengers were interviewed at BAA's airports at a cost for fieldwork of £46,000.

13.14. The items covered by the surveys were:

Facilities, services and conditions included in
passenger opinion survey

Facilities

Road access by private car	Telephones
On-airport car parks	Toilets
	Seating
Porters	
Trolleys	Bank/bureau de change
Left-luggage	Landside shops
Travellators	Landside catering (by specified outlets)
Lifts	Security
Escalators	
	Loudspeaker announcements
Departure TV screens	
Departure boards	
BAA information desk	

Conditions

Crowding (at check-in, in eating areas, elsewhere)	General airport appearance
	Ease of finding one's way
Walking distances	

Passenger service monitoring

13.15. Associated with but distinct from passenger opinions surveys is the monitoring of passenger service. Following pilot surveys approved by the Board in May 1983, the Board decided in February 1984 that routine monitoring should be carried out in 1984 on three aspects of service:

(*a*) check-in queueing times;

(*b*) departure lounge occupancies; and

(*c*) time to reach arrivals concourse.

13.16. Based on this research, the Board decided in April 1985 that routine passenger service monitoring for 1985 should be carried out only for the total time to reach the arrivals concourse. It was also decided to investigate further the connection between airlines' procedures and the length of check-in queues, and to monitor passengers' views on the subject. A separate research exercise is also being carried out in 1985 to develop a system for measuring automatically the occupancies of departure lounges.

Performance targets and indicators

13.17. Several performance indicators are reported to the Board at quarterly intervals. The indicators most relevant to commercial activities are:

duty- and tax-free income per international departing passenger (IDP);
other concession income per passenger;
gross property income; and
complaints per 100,000 passengers.

Other Trading research

13.18. BAA told us that it undertakes specific market research in all major areas of its retailing activity, and investigates customer attitudes both to the goods and services which are currently provided and to those which might be introduced. It also interviews non-purchasers in order to investigate their reasons for not buying, and undertakes research into pricing issues by examining, for example, passengers' awareness of duty- and tax-free prices. BAA has also commissioned outside consultants to develop a price information system to permit the monitoring of prices of BAA's primary duty- and tax-free products in relation to BAA's most important competitors: airlines, other airports, domestic and international 'High Streets' and a cross-channel ferry. This complements BAA's existing six-monthly price surveys which are the basis for determining prices in duty- and tax-free shops. A list of the High Street shops covered by these surveys is displayed at or near the entrance to each duty-free shop. Price tags on some products state the saving on the High Street price.

Service standards built into concession terms

13.19. BAA is committed to encouraging improvements in service standards offered to its customers by its trading concessionaires. As far as the Authority thinks possible, the standards of service required from concessionaires are specified in concession contracts. In retail contracts, for example, the concessionaire is required to stock specified brand leaders, to operate in such a way as to maximise turnover, to open at set hours dictated by passenger traffic and to staff at a level that does not cause the public undue waiting. Tenders for concessions have to include details of staff training programmes. For catering similar service and price level provisions are made. In addition, product specifications for many 'core' products are included in the contract (for example, tea, coffee, pastries, sandwiches, alcohol and soft drinks).

Monitoring of standards built into concession agreements

13.20. Individual Product Managers in the Trading Department monitor some aspects of the standard of service, for example range of goods, price control, quality control of catering products and marketing activities.

13.21. Terminal Management staff at the individual airports, on behalf of the Trading Department, carry out day-to-day monitoring of standards of service on such matters as specified opening hours, cleaning, numbers and quality of uniformed staff; they also check levels of stock and other matters. Inspections at each shop are usually made once or twice per Duty Manager shift.

---

[1]BAA Annual Report and Accounts, 1984–85, page 62, paragraph 34.

Staff campaigns

13.22. BAA has mounted ' Please the Passenger' and similar staff campaigns, both for BAA and, in collaboration with concessionaires, for concession staff. A total of some 3,400 BAA staff have attended the two and half hour Phase I session of the ' Please the Passenger' programme. In the period October 1984 to March 1985, more than 1,000 staff attended the two-day 'Face to Face' programme. To date some 2,000 staff have seen the video programme 'Points of View'. BAA intends that by the end of 1985 all BAA staff will have seen the video.

Signposting

13.23. Signposting at airports has recently been reviewed by BAA with the intention of simplifying the standard system by separating directional and commercial signs, so reducing the number of main direction signs. At Heathrow's Terminal 3, for example, arriving international passengers are at present faced by 237 signs. (BAA told us that this number includes signs with a wide variety of purposes: 'No entry', exit signs, facilities signs on doors, statutory notices, escape route signs, mandatory signs, and commercial and fascia signs.) We understand that BAA's signposting policy will continue to be based on the BAA Signs Manual as amended by the 1985 review, the principles of which were set by the Executive.

13.24. In its ' Please the Passenger' campaign for staff, BAA refers to the stress suffered by passengers at airports. We understand, however, that BAA has made no formal study of this subject. Judgment is necessarily subjective as to whether or to what extent passengers are under stress, or whether the provision of particular commercial facilities tends to increase or reduce this.

Trading journal

13.25. The free publication *Trading Post* is intended to increase staff awareness of the need for service to the public. Thirteen thousand copies are printed each month. Ten thousand copies are distributed with *Airport News* to the airports. Three thousand copies are taken by Trading Department.

Airport Consultative Committees

13.26. Under section 2 of the Airports Authority Act 1975 BAA is required to provide adequate consultation facilities for, *inter alia,* the users and nearby residents of its seven airports. At each airport there is a Consultative Committee whose roles include:

(a) the provision of a means for BAA to consult airport users and others;

(b) the promotion of the airport; and

(c) the provision of an alternative channel for passenger comments and complaints.

The last role is the particular responsibility at each airport of the Passenger Services sub-Committee or Group.

13.27. The airport Consultative Committees were established by BAA, which appoints the chairmen and pays them honoraria. Secretariat staff and facilities may be paid for by BAA or by local authorities. As noted in paragraph 13.7 the Passenger Services sub-Committee at each airport receives a monthly summary of comments on Comment Cards. Results of passenger opinion surveys are not reported to the Committees.

13.28. For BAA as a whole there is a Consultation Co-ordinating Council to facilitate consultation between BAA and airlines. It meets twice a year.

Results of service monitoring

Complaints

13.29. Each Monthly Management Report to the BAA Board contains an analysis of comments received for the month in question, a comparison with the same month in the previous year and a longer-term trend. Twice yearly there is also a more detailed breakdown of comments by specific categories. The Monthly Management Report for December 1984, tabled at the meeting of the Board in February 1985, summarised complaints/compliments at each airport in December 1983 and December 1984:

| | December 1983 | | December 1984 | |
	Complaints	Compliments	Complaints	Compliments
Heathrow	194	46	164	45
Gatwick	35	41	56	47
Stansted	2	10	3	2
Glasgow	15	4	18	9
Edinburgh	9	9	14	7
Prestwick	1	1	2	2
Aberdeen	3	0	4	2

The main causes of the increase from 35 to 56 complaints at Gatwick were Left Luggage (from 1 to 8), Facilities—seating and decor (from 2 to 6) and Other Facilities (from 6 to 13). Between December 1983 and December 1984 the number of passengers increased by 9 per cent at Heathrow, by 12 per cent at Gatwick, and by 21 per cent at Edinburgh. Complaints per 100,000 passengers averaged eight over the first nine months of 1984–85 compared with a targeted maximum of 15.

Performance indicators

13.30. Other performance indicators in the December 1984 Monthly Management Report covered duty- and tax-free income per IDP, other concession income per passenger, and gross property income. For 1984–85 the final results showed an increase in duty- and tax-free income per IDP of 5·7 per cent compared with a target of 7·5 per cent. For other concession income per passenger the target of 3·5 per cent was exactly met. Property income increased by 16 per cent compared with a target of 10 per cent.

Service standards

13.31. At its meeting in April 1985 the Board noted the following check-in queueing times at Heathrow (all three terminals), Gatwick and Glasgow revealed by surveys undertaken in busy periods during June to September 1984:

		Check-in queueing times Minutes	
	Average	95% queueing time*	Maximum
Heathrow Terminal 1	4·3	13	44
Heathrow Terminal 2	5·4	17	47
Heathrow Terminal 3	7·4	24	55
Gatwick	6·5	23	70
Glasgow	5·7	20	47

* 95 per cent queueing times indicate that 5 per cent of passengers experienced longer times.

During the busy periods surveyed the lowest average queueing time was at Heathrow Terminal 1 (4·3 minutes) and the highest average at Heathrow Terminal 3 (7·4 minutes); five per cent of the passengers at Heathrow Terminal 1 queued for longer than 13 minutes, and five per cent of the passengers at Heathrow Terminal 3 had to wait longer than 24 minutes. BAA told us that this has led to the further research in this area outlined in paragraph 13.16.

Passenger opinion surveys

13.32. From the first quarter's results of continuous monitoring BAA concluded that only a small percentage of passengers using facilities and services expressed dissatisfaction with them. Baggage trolleys and catering created the highest volume of dissatisfaction. At all locations except Stansted the level of dissatisfied users of catering was between 17 per cent and 33 per cent. (At Stansted the relatively small proportion of passengers using the landside bar/buffet made no complaints.) Most satisfactory to passengers were the speed and thoroughness of security checks, general airport appearance, and the 'ease of finding one's way'.

13.33. The survey of duty-free shopping July 1983 to June 1984 produced detailed results for each of Heathrow's three terminals and each of the other six BAA airports. The figures for usage and 'never buy duty-free' at Heathrow Terminal 1, for example, were as follows:

	Usage (passengers buying duty-free)	Passengers who never buy duty-free
Heathrow Terminal 1	41–48% (range over four quarters)	9%

13.34. The January 1985 catering survey was conducted at Heathrow, Gatwick, Glasgow, Edinburgh and Aberdeen:

Proportion of respondents who used catering

per cent

	January 1984	July 1984	January 1985
Heathrow Terminal 1	62	63	59
Heathrow Terminal 2	65	65	69
Heathrow Terminal 3	64	67	70
Gatwick	65	69	66
Aberdeen	63	68	64
Glasgow	69	68	57
Edinburgh	58	61	50

The heading which attracted most complaint from respondents at all terminals was ' value for money '; 33 per cent at Edinburgh and Gatwick thought the range of food could be increased; and at Edinburgh 39 per cent thought prices were too high while 22 per cent criticised the quality of food.

13.35. The March 1985 survey of duty-paid shops showed that:

(a) 53 per cent of the total sample had bought or intended to buy from the Skyshop or other duty-paid shop, with the most frequent purchases being:

	%
Newspapers	50
Magazines	25
Confectionery	24
Paperback books	17

(b) Passengers were asked to give a mark (1 being ' very poor ', 3 ' average ' and 5 ' very good '); the average of responses was:

Cleanliness	4·23
Friendliness of staff	3·70
Speed of service	3·77
Range of goods	3·75
Range of shops	3·56
Prices	3·55

Conclusions

13.36. BAA considers that in the medium to long term the maintenance or increase of commercial revenue is an indication of satisfactory commercial service. We accept that where increases in commercial revenue do not result from higher prices (in real terms), but from an increase in the goods and services bought per passenger, that is one indication that passengers are finding those goods and services attractive.

13.37. Underlying the figures for commercial revenue as a whole, however, there may be significant differences in the quality of service associated with various commercial activities. BAA must therefore continue to look separately at the individual performance of specific activities.

13.38. BAA is placing increasing emphasis, in its monitoring of commercial services, on passenger opinion surveys. The results of these should be made available, as a matter of routine, to the Passenger Services sub-Committee at each airport.

13.39. Provision should continue to be made for the representation of passengers' interests by such Passenger Services sub-Committees. Given the variety of roles which an airport Consultative Committee as a whole is required to play, including acting as a means for BAA to consult the residents of areas near the airport, and the promotion of the airport, consideration should be given to increasing the independence of the Passenger Services sub-Committees by separating their funding and the appointment of their members from those of the Consultative Committees.

3162890 I

CHAPTER 14

Overall assessment: the public interest: summary of conclusions: the future

Overall assessment

14.1. In the management of its affairs the British Airports Authority is continually faced with the need to decide between competing demands for limited facilities. All managers face such choices, but they are particularly frequent and difficult in the management of airports. The major airports inherited by the Authority are so sited that it is difficult to extend them (even if it were environmentally acceptable and economically sound so to do). All the Authority's airports were designed when air travel was the province of the few rather than the many, and the design and layout frequently inhibit development or expansion of the facilities (as in the Central Terminal Area at Heathrow). The growing demands on space in terminal buildings for operational use—for security, Customs and Immigration, the movement of passengers and their baggage—must be reconciled with each other and with the demands on space for commercial activities. The Chairman of the Authority told us

... the duty ... to provide proper facilities at the airports for passengers and cargo shippers must take precedence over commercial activities. Where considerations of space are concerned, commercial activities must take second place.

We believe that this attitude should be maintained in the future, particularly given the temptation which is likely to arise to put greater emphasis on commercial activities. However, the choice between operational and commercial needs is not black and white. Many commercial activities, although not strictly a pre-requisite for the safe and efficient movement of passengers, are seen by them as a basic necessity. It is commonplace that, as standards of living improve, yesterday's luxury becomes tomorrow's necessity. Air travellers in 1985 expect as a matter of course to find at an airport some catering and shopping facilities as well as adequate waiting areas and toilets. At the larger airports they will expect to find banking facilities, duty- and tax-free shops, and facilities for hiring a car and booking accommodation. The Chairman told us

It is very difficult to draw a line ... I cannot conceive that we could ever build an airport without certain commercial facilities which the average passenger today would demand ... So what are the basic requirements, and what are passengers' reasonable requirements, and what extra you provide is all very difficult to define, and it is changing all the time ... the nature of the traffic and ... the nature of the passengers and their requirements and their perception of what they ought to have, in five years in civil aviation changes dramatically.

14.2. It must also be borne in mind that those very circumstances which make it difficult to reconcile competing demands also provide an opportunity for exploitation. While in theory certain parts of an airport are open to all, it would

126

not be sensible to encourage people not involved in air travel to visit it in large numbers: to do so could seriously impede operations. The airside of an airport is accessible only to passengers and those who work there. Only passengers departing on international flights have access to airside duty- and tax-free shops. In practice an airport constitutes a closed market, in which monopolistic exploitation would be practicable.

14.3. These general considerations must be borne in mind in any attempt to assess how well—or badly—the Authority carries on its commercial activities. We have dealt in Chapter 4 with the difficulties of measuring performance by the available statistics, and we concluded there (paragraph 4.31) that the evidence is persuasive only in the case of rents. In this area, judged by comparisons made at Heathrow (which accounts for 72 per cent of the Authority's revenue from rents and services to tenants) the Authority can be seen to have done a little better than property owners generally, but not to such an extent as to justify any conclusion that it is abusing its monopoly position. For other sources of commercial revenue, movements in the figures over the past ten years can be largely if not wholly explained by extrinsic influences, and therefore provide no safe ground for assessing the Authority's performance. We must perforce make a more subjective judgment. This we base on all we have seen and heard during our inquiry: on our visits—and the visits of our staff—to the Authority's airports, and to a number of airports managed by local authorities: on our evaluation of the written and oral evidence given by the Authority and others and on our favourable assessment of the Authority's officers concerned with commercial affairs whom we met. We also bear in mind the limited range and extent of those matters about which, in the preceding chapters, we have been critical and have put forward suggestions for improvement. Taking all these together, it is our conclusion that the Authority has shown a generally satisfactory standard of performance of its commercial activities, although there is room for improvement.

The public interest

14.4. Our terms of reference require us to consider whether, in relation to its commercial activities (excluding the application of the Authority's commercial revenues to finance non-commercial activities), the Authority is pursuing a course of conduct which operates against the public interest. The Act[1] specifies three heads under which such a course of conduct could arise:

(a) Efficiency and costs. We have set out above our general conclusion that the Authority's standard of performance (ie efficiency) is satisfactory. We have not had any evidence to suggest that overall the Authority's costs could be materially reduced. We do not believe the Authority's attitude towards costs is such as to lead it into a course of conduct which operates against the public interest.

(b) The service provided. We have pointed out several ways in which the service provided by the Authority in its commercial activities can be improved, particularly in relation to competition, but we received only a small number of complaints about it.

(c) Possible abuse of a monopoly situation. The danger is real: and in a closed market such as is found at an airport there is always bound to be some

---

[1]Section 11(1) Competition Act 1980.

127

suspicion of exploitation. However, while we have reservations about the Authority's attitude to competition, we do not think that so far it is acting in disregard of its duty as a public body.

We conclude that while there is scope for improvement in the service provided by the Authority in its commercial activities it is not, in relation to those activities, pursuing a course of conduct which operates against the public interest.

Summary of conclusions

14.5. Our terms of reference require us to consider whether, in relation to its commercial activities, the Authority could improve its efficiency, or reduce its costs, or improve the service provided, with particular reference to:

(a) the scope for increasing competition at the point of sale, having regard to security and safety requirements and the need to ensure the comfort and convenience of passengers and the efficient operation of the airport;

(b) the methods and practices of the Authority in selecting the persons to whom concessions are to be granted including the Authority's procedures for inviting and accepting tenders, the imposition on concessionaires by the Authority of contractual terms relating to the price, nature, range and quality of the goods and services to be provided by concessionaires and the award and renewal by the Authority of contracts;

(c) the monitoring and control by the Authority of the standard of services provided to passengers by concessionaires;

(d) the administration and management by the Authority of leases of land where the Authority is the lessor.

The extent to which the Authority could in our judgment improve its efficiency, reduce its costs or improve the service it provides appears from our conclusions in Chapters 4 to 13, of which the following is a summary.

Summary of Conclusions

Recommendation Number		Paragraph Number
	The role of the BAA Board	
1.	BAA encourages its part-time Board members to take an interest in specific activities according to their individual expertise and experience. There is at present no member with retailing experience, despite the scale of BAA's commercial activities. **An increase in the size of the Board would give an opportunity to appoint such a member. We recommend such a change.**	5.44
2.	**The Board should, in approaching a decision on the provision and allocation of space in new and redeveloped terminals, tell the Executive what range of options should be considered, and require the Executive to demonstrate that the full range of commercial possibilities, within the constraints imposed by physical conditions, has been explored.**	5.45

Planning Guidelines

3.   **Planning Guidelines, which are currently being updated after seven years, should be updated more frequently. Care should be taken to ensure that they are appropriate to facilities on the scale likely to be planned.**   5.46

Targets

4.   **The Board will be able to set feasible but more challenging targets for commercial performance for the year ensuing if it can achieve greater understanding of the relative roles of, on the one hand, managerial effectiveness and other factors largely under BAA's control, and, on the other hand, those external factors which are largely outside its control.**   5.47

Organisation

The organisational changes resulting from 'Chewton Glen' reinforced BAA's trend towards decentralisation, with the exception of the new arrangements for the organisation of commercial functions which went against this trend. On BAA's own admission, it is too early to be sure that the new commercial organisation fulfils Chewton Glen's hopes. Accepting that, the Chewton Glen decision on commercial matters seems to us to have been soundly based.   5.48

5.   In setting up the Trading Department, the Commercial Development Director has given priority to the retailing activities at terminals. **In due course it will be necessary to ensure that the potential of other commercial activities including, for example, car parks, cargo and property receives the attention already given to retailing.**   5.49

6.   The division of responsibility for commercial performance between the Trading Department and the airport managements is currently being debated within BAA. We consider that the present arrangements are satisfactory. **The Commercial Development Director should retain his responsibility for advising BAA on the exploitation of all commercial potential, and the Director or General Manager of an airport should have final responsibility for all activities at his airport.**   5.50

Information and computing

BAA has in recent years noted deficiencies in the management information relevant to its commercial activities and has developed, or begun to develop, new systems to remedy these deficiencies.   6.30

Continuing difficulties with the property system suggest that not all the problems identified in the 1983 review of the whole of the Authority's information processing strategy have been solved.   6.31

At an early stage in our inquiry the Authority admitted to 'serious...concern' over its new computerised property management system. From BAA's own statement on the present position past mistakes are evident, and most important and urgent decisions, particularly concerning Heathrow, remain to be taken. BAA is now seeking information about computerised property management systems recently developed elsewhere.   6.32

7.   In view of our proposal that final responsibility for all activities at an airport, including Trading and other commercial activities, should remain with its Director or General Manager, **it will be**

necessary to ensure that the new computerised Trading Information System meets the specific requirements of the airport management responsible for Trading performance.

6.33

Finance

BAA did not achieve the targets set for it by the Government for the period 1980–81 to 1982–83, when traffic growth was less than had been expected. It expects to achieve the targets set for the period 1983–84 to 1985–86.

7.52

Budgets

8.

The fact that the Authority has exceeded its concession income budgets and kept within its expenditure budgets during recent years may suggest that its budgets should be made more rigorous and challenging. **We recommend that it reviews its budget-setting procedures accordingly.**

7.53

Presentation of results

A substantial proportion of the Authority's expenditure is not directly attributable to particular activities and an element of judgment therefore enters into the allocation of that expenditure, which may affect the extent to which the reported results for each activity are meaningful. BAA told us that this would not affect its traffic charges but we nevertheless consider it important that the Authority's results from particular activities at different airports should be reported more accurately and as clearly as possible. The Authority is making changes to this end, particularly in the development of its new 'general ledger' management accounting and information system. We accept that the Authority is correct to treat expenditure on such items as terminal concourses, roads and airport administration as wholly attributable to traffic operations even though the first two are also used to give access to commercial facilities. To do otherwise would imply that commercial activities were of comparable significance to the Authority's primary objective to operate, plan and develop its airports so that air travellers and cargo may pass through safely, swiftly and as conveniently as possible.

7.54–7.59

9.

We consider that a distinction can and should continue to be drawn in the Authority's accounts between the results of its traffic operations and its commercial activities at each airport. This should continue to apply if privatisation takes place, so that the extent of subsidisation of traffic operations by commercial activities and of one airport by another is disclosed.

7.59, 7.60

10.

We recommend that the Authority should show separately in its published accounts for particular activities at airports the contribution made by each activity first to the Authority's non-specific expenditure and profits and overhead expenditure and secondly to the Authority's trading profits or losses after deducting from those contributions an allocation of its non-specific expenditure made on a 'best judgment' basis together with an explanation of the basis used.

7.61

Internal audit

11.

While we have no reason to believe that posts in the internal audit branch are not correctly graded, **we hope that the Authority will keep** under careful review the grading of internal audit staff, including the Chief Internal Auditor, so that the branch can operate effectively and carry appropriate weight in its dealings with operational management.

7.62

12.

We found the general organisation and operation of the internal audit function to be satisfactory (although response times were tending to lengthen). But the efficiency of internal audit depends not only on a sound structure but on continued support being given by the Managing Director and senior management. **We therefore consider it desirable that the Chief Internal Auditor should report directly to a Board member. The Audit Committee should become more closely involved in overseeing the internal audit function.**

7.63

Investment appraisal

Our examination of the appraisal of a number of investment projects indicates that the majority of investments have been subject to formal investment appraisal. The recent adoption of revised guidelines for project assessment should, however, lead to some improvement in the techniques of investment appraisal, particularly as applied to smaller projects.

8.21

In particular, the standard of investment appraisal should benefit from a wider quantification of available options; from a greater use of sensitivity analysis; from a more systematic assessment of non-financial benefits; and from a regular programme of back-checks as proposed in the revised guidelines.

8.22

13.

No separate appraisal is carried out of the commercial content of the major 'combined' investments. BAA argued that options for provision of commercial facilities have been constrained by the nature of the sites available. We believe this argument can be overstated. **Where there are options for the provision of commercial facilities in these major developments, these options also should be subjected to a formal economic appraisal.**

8.23

Concessions

14.

Five-year contracts may not be in the best interests of the concessionaires; nevertheless, given the nature of the monopoly rights granted by BAA, **we think that all contracts should remain subject to regular tendering.**

9.24

15.

We consider that the question of capital investment by catering concessionaires should be kept under review in the light of the outcome of BAA's recent proposals to provide them with a greater incentive.

9.24

Property management

Examination of files and discussions with airport staff showed that the policies and procedures for leasing were being followed in detail.

10.29

Present vacant office accommodation at Heathrow and Gatwick represents a small proportion of total office accommodation at the two airports, and is projected by BAA to be fully absorbed within five years. The increase in rents at Heathrow has been greater than the national average and the level of rents at the airport is generally above that in surrounding areas. BAA policy for determining rental levels appears reasonable.

10.30, 10.31

Aircraft fuel supply

The new fuel agreement at Heathrow makes provision for the entry of new suppliers to the hydrant consortium. It will be easier to judge the effectiveness of this provision when the result of British Airways' application to join the consortium is known. **BAA should increase competition in the supply of fuel at Gatwick when the present fuel arrangements are re-negotiated.**

16.

10.32

Competition

The extent of competition at point of sale is limited by the lack of space within the airport terminals.[1] Nevertheless even where competition would be possible, either directly or through promotional activities, BAA effectively restricts or prevents it. BAA believes that it has an obligation to offer a considerable degree of protection to concessionaires who, through competitive tendering, have won the right to trade. BAA also believes that consumer choice is better secured through a variety of products for sale than through duplication of suppliers and tries to ensure by price regulation and other controls over concessionaires that customers get value for money.

11.66, 11.67

We do not find these arrangements fully effective. In order to increase competition **we recommend that the Authority:**

11.67

17.   (*a*) **continues to make every effort to attract a greater range of tenderers with a view to reducing the present concentration of concessions among a small number of firms, and thus providing a better spread of experience on which to judge concessionaires' performance;**

11.68

18.   (*b*) **should seek to ensure that full information is provided at the outset, and that the time allowed for the preparation of the tenders is adequate for new tenderers;**

11.69

19.   (*c*) **should allow Skyshop concessionaires to trade under their own names in the interests of staff motivation and customer service;**

11.70

20.   (*d*) **should review the terms of its car hire concessions to ensure that customers are charged on a basis appropriate to the type of hire involved;**

11.71

21.   (*e*) **should facilitate competition in car rentals, allow off-airport car hire operators to advertise without discrimination and provide adequate generic signposting and coach pick-up facilities;**

11.71

22.   (*f*) **should cease its present practice of discriminating against advertisements at its airports for off-airport competitors to its concessionaires;**

11.72

23.   (*g*) **should arrange matters so that in any Heathrow terminal an airline without rights to handle its own traffic has a choice of at least two handlers neither of which is an airline with which it is in direct competition;**

11.75

24.   (*h*) **should, in determining the arrangements for ground handling at Heathrow, not limit its consideration to airlines with existing self-handling rights and should take account of the charges made to airlines and the cost savings achievable;**

11.75

---

[1]The Chairman said, however, he hoped that in the development of Terminal 4 at Heathrow enough space would be available, for the first time, to introduce competition in catering. When our report was nearly complete BAA told us that all the catering outlets in Terminal 4 had nevertheless been let to a single concessionaire, who does not hold a catering concession at any other BAA airport.

25.   (*i*)   should, on the expiry of the present Aer Lingus contract, open the opportunity to tender for the position of nominated handler to any airline using Heathrow (whether or not that airline currently has handling rights) and to any outside handling agency;   11.76

26.   (*j*)   should allow airlines with handling rights at Heathrow to undertake business in any terminal, particularly where this would improve utilisation of equipment: to this end the Authority should survey with the Airline Operators Committee the utilisation of equipment and staff at Heathrow and the charges made; and   11.77

27.   (*k*)   should take advantage of the opening of the North Terminal at Gatwick to invite tenders for additional handlers and should establish the degree of choice set out in (*g*) above.   11.78

Basis of tendering

The general form of a concession and the basis upon which tenders are judged benefits BAA rather than the consumer. This is consistent with the Authority's policy to maximise revenue but may not be consistent with its obligations as a public enterprise. An alternative approach might be to let concession contracts on a different basis, for example a fixed rental and prescribed standards of service, tenders being judged on the lowest prices proposed to be charged to customers.   11.79

Air traffic services

It might be difficult to introduce a contractor other than the CAA in the London area. **We recommend, in view of the potential reduction in costs to airlines, that the Authority should consider employing another contractor at its smaller airports.**   4.30

28.

Manpower efficiency

It has not been possible to apportion accurately the man-hours spent on commercial activities but we have seen no evidence of over- or under-staffing. We are satisfied that the downward pressure on staffing stemming from performance targets has been effective. Our judgment is that there is a high level of expertise and effectiveness among BAA's staff responsible for its commercial activities.   12.21

Staff training

The Authority has devoted considerable resources to staff training during the past three years. **We hope that it will be able to carry out an objective assessment of the effects of this training.**   12.22

29.

Industrial relations

BAA has a satisfactory industrial relations system and we have been aware of a feeling of common purpose among all staff engaged in commercial activities.   12.23

Quality of service

BAA considers that in the medium to long term the maintenance or increase of commercial revenue is an indication of satisfactory service. We accept that an increase in such revenue resulting from an increase in the goods and services bought per passenger is one indication that passengers find those goods and services attractive.   13.36

Recommendation Number		Paragraph Number
30.	The quality of service associated with specific commercial activities may differ significantly. **BAA must therefore continue to look separately at the individual performance of specific activities.**	13.37

Performance indicators

31.	Available statistics do not provide a satisfactory guide to BAA's performance of its commercial activities. **We recommend that further effort should be devoted to the establishment of meaningful performance indicators.**	4.31, 4.32 4.33
32.	BAA is placing increasing emphasis, in its monitoring of commercial services, on passenger opinion surveys. **The results of these should be made available, as a matter of routine, to the Passenger Services sub-Committee at each airport.**	13.38
33. 34.	**Passenger Services sub-Committees should continue to represent passengers' interests.** Given the variety of roles which an airport Consultative Committee is required to play, **consideration should be given to increasing the independence of the Passenger Services sub-Committees by separating their funding and the appointment of members from those of the Consultative Committees.**	13.39

The future

14.6. We have examined the Authority as it has been and as it is now, and our recommendations for change relate to the present organisation. We cannot, however, ignore the announced policy of the present Government to bring about a major change by the early privatisation of the Authority. Indeed, this policy was translated into a detailed programme of action in the White Paper 'Airports Policy'[1] published on 5 June 1985 during the course of our inquiry. We have therefore thought it right to examine our recommendations in the light of the White Paper. As a result, we have concluded that, although they are made in respect of the existing organisation, we have no reason to believe that the general sense of our recommendations will be found inapplicable to the new organisation envisaged.

14.7. The captive nature of the concessionaires' market, and the airlines' pressure to maintain the existing degree of cross-subsidy between commercial and non-commercial activities, already encourage the Authority to exploit its commercial opportunities. While it is not for us to comment on the new arrangements proposed in the White Paper, we think it right to draw attention to the additional pressures which might be generated by the search for a high rate of return to shareholders in the new enterprise: pressures which will make it even more difficult for the Authority's successor to hold a proper balance between an entrepreneurial approach to commercial activities and a possible abuse of a monopoly position.[2]

---

[1]Cmnd 9542.
[2]BAA told us that its commercial activities were not being affected by the prospect of privatisation. The Authority did express concern about the demands for operational space posed by the continuous and rapid growth of passenger numbers. The Managing Director told us he was '... very worried about the huge surge of passenger traffic which we are experiencing ... The balance ... is, if anything, stacked against the ability for commercial activities to get into new areas or new parts of the airport ... Given our prime responsibility is the processing of passengers and freight and airlines, if there is ... a conflict it may well be that we will have to cut back on some of the space allocated to commercial activities'. However, another strand of thought about the future appears in the Trading Department's Marketing Plan Summary 1985: 'it is a safe assumption that' privatisation 'will result in an increased prominence of the profit-earning commercial functions'.

J G LE QUESNE *(Chairman)*

PATRICIA MANN

B C OWENS

J S SADLER

D P THOMSON

Professor K D George, being a member of the Group, dissents from the conclusions for the reason set out in this report

N E D BURTON *(Secretary)*

2 September 1985

Note of Dissent

by Professor K D George

I agree with the conclusions that have been arrived at by my colleagues except with respect to one matter, which is the public interest finding on the way in which BAA has effectively restricted or prevented competition to its concessionaires even where such competition would be possible. I conclude that in this respect the Authority has been pursuing a course of conduct that operates against the public interest. A partial remedy of the situation would be for BAA to be obliged to implement the relevant recommendations made in this report.

K D GEORGE
2 September 1985

APPENDIX 2.1
(referred to in paragraph 2.5)

Interested third parties

†Aberdeen Airport Consultative Committee
 Aerodrome Owners Association
 Air Transport Operators Association
*Allders Ltd
†American Express Europe Ltd
 Association of British Travel Agents
 Association of Suppliers to Airlines, Airports & Shipping
*Avis Rent A Car Ltd
†Birmingham Airport
 Britannia Airways Ltd
*British Airports Authority Trade Union Side
*British Airways plc
*British Caledonian Airways Ltd
 British Civil Aviation Standing Conference
*British Midland Airways Ltd
 British Ports Association
 British Tourist Authority
 British Vehicle Rental and Leasing Association
*Civil Aviation Authority
 Consumers' Association
 Cormack (Aircraft Services) Ltd
 Dan-Air Services Ltd
*Department of Trade and Industry
*Department of Transport
†East Midlands Airport
†Euro Car Parks
 Falcon Jet Centre Ltd
†Gatwick Airport Consultative Committee
 Gatwick Car Facilities Association
 Gatwick Resident Airline Operators Association
 General Aviation Manufacturers and Traders Association
†Glasgow Airport Consultative Committee
 Heathrow Airport Airline Operators Committee
*Heathrow Airport Consultative Committee
 Heathrow Hydrant Consortium
 Heavylift Cargo Airlines Ltd
 Hertz Rent A Car
 London Borough of Hillingdon
 Institute of Purchasing and Supply
 Joint Airports Committee of Local Authorities
†Leeds/Bradford Airport
 London Chamber of Commerce and Industry

---

* Attended hearing at the Commission.
† Discussed evidence with Commission staff.

†Luton Airport
†Manchester International Airport
 Massetts Lodge
 National Consumer Council
†Newcastle Airport
†Pan American World Airways Inc
*Periodical Publishers Association:
    Business Press International Ltd
    Haymarket Publishing Ltd
    IPC Magazines Ltd
    Magnum Distribution Ltd
    John Menzies plc
    New Statesman Distribution Ltd
    W H Smith & Son Ltd
 Prestwick Airport Consultative Committee
 Spelthorne Borough Council
 Stansted Airport Consultative Committee
 Swan National Ltd
*Town and Country Car Rental
 Tradewinds Airways Ltd
*Trusthouse Forte plc
 The Windmill Group

---

* Attended hearing at the Commission.
† Discussed evidence with Commission staff.

BAA airports compared with some other major airports

'000

	ATMs		Terminal passengers		International passengers		Cargo (tonnes)	
	1983	1984	1983	1984	1983	1984	1983	1984
Heathrow	260·1	274·1	26,749	29,147	22,351	24,096	469·7	544·0
Gatwick	134·7	141·0	12,477	13,954	11,446	12,817	109·6	146·3
Stansted	8·3	12·8	342	527	330	493	18·0	14·6
South-East	403·1	427·9	39,568	43,628	34,127	37,406	597·3	704·9
Prestwick	4·1	3·1	250	235	245	230	10·5	10·0
Edinburgh	28·6	34·6	1,276	1,491	262	260	0·8	0·8
Glasgow	54·5	55·1	2,443	2,747	1,005	1,179	11·5	15·6
Aberdeen—fixed wing	38·0	35·9	1,094	1,093	195	187	3·7	4·0
Aberdeen—helicopters	44·5	46·2	644	666	—	—	4·1	4·4
Total BAA	572·8	602·8	45,275	49,860	35,834	39,262	627·9	739·7
Other UK airports								
Manchester	64·5	70·3	5,087	5,960	3,987	4,682	24·5	28·7
Jersey	50·3	51·6	1,385	1,436	41	33	6·8	7·6
Birmingham	32·1	35·1	1,560	1,693	1,200	1,304	3·3	4·5
Belfast	31·3	33·5	1,389	1,580	245	285	18·7	24·4
US airports								
Atlanta	573·4	648·2	37,920	38,989	1,214	1,375	307·2	311·7
Chicago	480·1	499·3	42,874	45,726	2,890	3,286	627·2	615·1
Los Angeles	441·6	474·9	33,426	34,362	4,910	5,383	698·7	767·3
Dallas/Ft Worth	412·5	501·8	26,786	32,267	1,937	1,313	238·3	283·7
Denver	383·3	447·1	25,247	28,576	273	230	141·1	141·8
New York/LGA	294·0	313·5	18,813	20,303	—	—	35·4	42·6
New York/JFK	286·8	291·6	27,904	29,935	14,666	16,334	1,039·4	1,120·7
European airports								
Frankfurt	207·7	212·4	17,030	18,319	12,360	13,390	649·2	731·9
Paris/Orly	152·7	153·8	16,258	17,174	6,846	7,311	164·3	205·2
Paris/CDG	130·7	133·5	13,411	13,628	11,692	12,123	497·9	506·4
Amsterdam	139·7	141·3	9,680	10,555	9,602	10,473	370·4	438·2

Source: BAA.

(referred to in paragraphs 3.23 and 3.25)

British Airports Authority: organisation chart

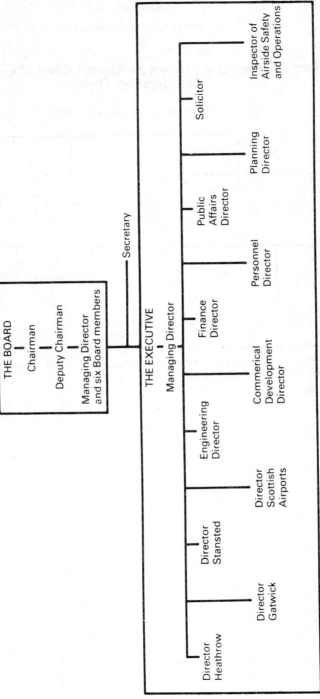

Note: This chart shows lines of responsibility and functions but not necessarily the relative status of individual posts.

Source: BAA.

Organisation chart showing responsibilities of Commercial Development Director

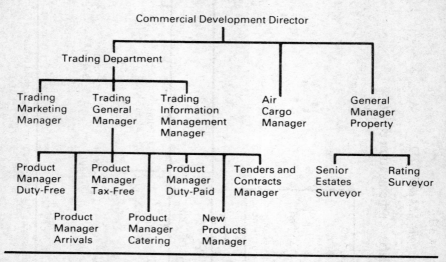

Note: This chart shows lines of responsibility and functions but not necessarily the relative status of individual posts.

Source: BAA.

Extract from 1985 Corporate Plan (policy section)

Commercial

6.14. To meet the needs of airport users for the provision of goods and services in such a way as to encourage a competitive and commercial approach and to ensure the effective utilisation of its assets and opportunities.

6.15. BAA is committed to the concept of maximum development of income from sources other than aircraft landing and parking fees and will aim to maximise profit in its commercial affairs, consistent with the need to maintain the credibility of its pricing structures on a long term basis and with its obligations as a public enterprise.

Trading

6.16. Of the facilities and services provided at airports, some are unique to the airport environment, such as ground handling of aircraft and air traffic control, whereas others, such as shops, banks and car parks, are common throughout the land. Since its formation in 1965 it has been BAA policy that the latter services should, wherever possible, be provided by specialist companies with proven commercial and operating experience, with the BAA providing essential airport services and facilities. This policy has had three main advantages:

    (i) It has introduced a significant element of competition into the provision of these services.

    (ii) It has enabled the passenger to benefit from the commercial expertise of the major private sector companies who have experience in the fields such as catering, retailing, car parking etc.

    (iii) It has enabled the BAA, a relatively small organisation, to concentrate its resources and expertise in the provision of essential airport facilities and services.

6.17. In pursuit of this policy, the BAA's commercial activities—including shops, restaurants, and car rental facilities—are operated by specialist private sector companies on the basis of competitively tendered concession contracts, whereby the BAA provides the basic accommodation and equipment, with the successful tenderer providing the staff, supplies and the service.

6.18. As a matter of policy, major contracts are awarded after competitive tender normally for a period of five years which, subject to performance and agreed terms, the Authority may extend for a further three years. This is regarded as a reasonable length of time for a concessionaire to become established and develop the business, whilst being sufficiently short to ensure a reasonable frequency of opportunity for new entrants to compete for concessions.

K

6.19. Having regard to its statutory duties under the terms of the Airports Authority Act 1975, the BAA cannot and indeed would not wish to abrogate its overall responsibilities for services to passengers and users of the airport. It is therefore the BAA's policy to maintain some degree of control over its commercial operations. For example, in respect of catering concessions, control is maintained over both price and quality and there is continuous day-to-day liaison between the concessionaires and the BAA to ensure that all aspects of the quality of service are maintained. Similar controls apply to other concessions, to ensure that passengers' needs are met in the most effective and economical way. BAA considers that the current arrangements offer the considerable advantage to passengers of the pooling of expertise by the BAA and the concessionaires.

6.20. Competitive tendering of relatively short contracts, and close involvement and control by BAA management therefore combine to ensure that specialist concessionaires compete to maintain high standards of service and efficiency for the benefit of customers.

6.21. It must be recognised, however, that space constraints are often paramount in the older terminal buildings, many of which simply do not have sufficient space for increased numbers of concessionaires to be accommodated. However, even where competing concessions are not possible there is nevertheless a very real element of competition, both in terms of the regular renewal of the contract and, often, competition with other companies off-airport, with other services, or with foreign airports and airlines. In view of the limited space available at airports, therefore, a balance must be maintained between choice and proliferation, and BAA believes that the existing situation provides the optimum commercial solution and therefore the most efficient use of facilities.

Property

6.22. BAA will continue to seek to provide sites and buildings at its airports for the use of airlines and others as part of its present duty to provide services and facilities. Market rents will continue to be charged. BAA will seek to balance that duty against the commercial objective of optimising rental returns against capital invested.

6.23. BAA will also continue to seek to minimise its liability for local authority rates, development land tax and compensation under Part 1 of the Land Compensation Act 1973.

Extract from 1985 Corporate Plan (strategy section)

COMMERCIAL

Commercial Development

11.1. Commercial Development is made up of three branches—Trading, Property and Cargo Development. The creation of a central Trading Department in 1984 was a major part of the continuing drive to boost commercial income. Operating from Head Office it now provides a central source of specialist skills to airports.

The Trading Department

11.2. The Trading Branch organisation provides classic ' brand ' management for each of the main product areas, a marketing function covering premises development and promotions and a market research and business intelligence section. By specialising in this manner the BAA is bringing to bear an increasingly professional and specialised approach to this vital area of its activities, and strategic Marketing Plans are being developed accordingly.

11.3. Trading is primarily concerned with profitably meeting the needs of passengers through retail activity at the separate airports. This will necessitate thorough training of Trading staff, frequent visits to all seven airports and good communications between locations.

11.4. Increased spend, and improvements in market penetration can only be achieved by the better identification and satisfaction of customer needs. In all areas of retailing, particularly in catering activities, this orientation forms a key part of the development programme.

11.5. Future improvements in income are also seen to come from a heightened awareness of market performance and trends and an increasing flexibility in taking advantage of these. There are opportunities for expansion both landside and airside through the introduction of new product offers, and the increased professionalism of current operations. More companies will be encouraged to tender for airport concessions as emphasis is placed on introducing specialist operators in some areas.

11.6. Whilst the main core of the business will continue to be the traditional Duty Free area, strong emphasis will also now be given to other areas. Overall, however, the greater part of medium term growth is seen as more likely to derive from increasing market penetration than from encouraging increases in average spend.

Duty and Tax Free Product Area

11.7. The major revenue earners are from Duty and Tax Free Trading. This will continue to be so. Actual penetration levels are such as to indicate the availability of further growth potential and this will be addressed in particular by stronger efforts to communicate the retail price advantage of duty free and also efforts to persuade non-buyers in the departures lounges to visit the shops.

11.8. The size of shops and the relative ratio between Duty and Tax Free are being addressed. Shop sizes will be increased wherever possible in overall terms and the proportion allocated to Tax Free increased. Opportunities have already been taken in Gatwick's South Terminal to implement this approach during 1984–85 and similar improvements will be made during the planning of the Heathrow Terminal 3 re-development scheme.

11.9. In Tax Free the introduction of wider product ranges and more individualistic style of presentation is taking place as opportunity presents itself.

11.10. The emphasis within Duty and Tax Free will be gradually transferred away from the established liquor market and declining tobacco market towards the Tax Free area and towards fragrances in particular where considerable growth potential is seen to exist.

Duty Paid Product Area

11.11. The Skyshops concept will continue to be progressively applied to Duty Paid outlets and income from these areas is forecast to increase significantly over the period of the Plan.

11.12. The fastest growth areas in the Duty Paid product area have been identified as Advertising Sales and Books, with significant real income growths forecast over the period of the Plan. Speciality retail shops are being introduced and are intended to provide an outlet for products which cannot be adequately marketed through the Skyshops. Despite the overlap between these two activities, the greater specialisation of such operators will provide a net gain to the Authority.

Arrivals Product Area

11.13. Car Rental is the priority area within the Arrivals Product Area and is indeed a priority within the whole Trading Marketing Plan. Income is forecast to grow, stimulated by a greater marketing effort, improved facilities for concessionaires, heightened value for money and the expansion of a number of services such as luxury car rental and chauffeur drive.

Catering Product Area

11.14. The approach towards catering on airport has been the subject of considerable innovation in a persistent endeavour to develop this activity. A heavy emphasis will be put on the identification of consumer needs, enhancement of design, flexibility, and satisfaction of market trends through improving quality, value and particularly service to customers.

General

11.15. The various product approaches must necessarily be backed up by aggressive advertising and promotional activity which will be tailored to the needs of individual product areas. The advertising of total airport offers will to some extent be taken off-airport to widen consumer awareness, whilst on the airports themselves the implementation of the Trading signage programme will be continued.

11.16. Emphasis will be placed upon creating distinctive, marketing-orientated premises to complement the product/service offer. The premises will reflect current consumer tastes and will be made as flexible in use as possible.

11.17. The increased involvement in commercial activities is necessitating the creation of a Trading Information System which will provide accurate, up-to-date, relevant information on trading results and buying patterns, in response to which customer needs can be more closely satisfied. This is anticipated to take at least one year to complete, although some parts of the overall system should be running earlier.

APPENDIX 5.3
(referred to in paragraphs 5.23 and 7.13)

BAA Corporate Plan — arrangements for its preparation

Introduction

1. Since its formation in 1965 the Authority has always had well developed physical planning procedures due to the long lead times involved in obtaining planning permission for airport facilities, their construction and commissioning. Prior to 1976, the Corporate Plan contained little more than the budget forecasts with no qualitative discussions of policies. In 1976, however, in anticipation of Government requirements, a more comprehensive Plan was drawn up, which has set the pattern for the on-going development of subsequent Plans.

2. In 1982, following a major internal re-appraisal of responsibilities and increased delegation of powers within the Authority, it was decided that the Corporate Planning Process should be expanded to become pro-active, a stronger stimulator of new ideas and develop further the options open to the business.

3. The Corporate Planning Process described below should be seen therefore as part of an evolving process which will undoubtedly be subject to further refinements over the next few years.

The Corporate Planning Process
Objectives/targets/traffic forecasts

4. At the start of the Corporate Planning cycle in May/June, the Authority agrees three major inputs: the objectives, the targets and the traffic forecasts. The objectives, which were formalised at the Government's request in 1982, are based upon the 1975 Airports Authority Act and are a statement of the overall framework within which the Authority operates. It is not expected that the objectives will alter much over time unless the 1975 Act is amended. The targets are a set of specific, quantified goals agreed with the Government to be achieved over a three year period.

5. The third major input is the forecasts of air traffic. The development and operation of airports is a highly capital intensive business with the investment risk lying in the fact that airport facilities can serve no purpose other than that for which they were originally intended, nor can they be easily disposed of or moved if they are created in the wrong manner. The planning timescale therefore has to reflect the long lead times involved in airport development—eight to ten years for a new terminal, for example, and at least 12 years for a new airport or a major expansion of an existing one.

6. It follows that long-term traffic forecasts are more than usually important to BAA and as a result considerable effort is expended to make them as realistic as possible. Forecasts of passenger throughput and aircraft movements and

146

cargo are prepared for each of the Authority's airports over the next 15 years apart from South East forecasts which are prepared on an aggregate basis after the first five years.

The appraisal meetings

7. The Corporate Planning Process itself begins annually in May/June when the Board formally agrees the objectives of the Authority, sets specific numeric profit, income and cost targets for the immediate future and highlights areas of the business requiring additional development within the period of the Corporate Plan. Also identified are a series of Policy Options looking at more radical aspects of the Business, some of which will be dealt with within the Plan, others which will be the subject of separate papers.

8. The Senior Directors and Managers then meet in July at a 'Corporate Appraisal' to learn the views of the Board and to agree the overall framework, assumptions and timetable for the preparation of Airport Business Plans. Agreement will also be reached at this stage on the input of Head Office departments, including for example Commercial Development, into the Business Planning process.

The Business Plans

9. In the development of an expanded and pro-active corporate planning process, two essential requirements have been kept to the fore: first, only those who manage the Authority's affairs are in a position to achieve the overall goals set out in the Corporate Plan; secondly, the planning process must recognise and support the thrust towards decentralisation and increased delegation of responsibility throughout the business.

10. The seven airports constitute discrete business units, operating within the framework of group policy determined by the Board in its centralised role. Each airport is therefore required to prepare and work to its own Business Plan, formulated by its own management, each year on the basis of the aforementioned corporate assumptions and guidelines agreed at the Corporate Appraisal Meeting in July.

11. Within each Airport Business Plan a series of 'Appraisal papers' are prepared for each major area of activity. These set specific objectives, give background information on current activity, provide detailed information on what is to be done over the five-year period of the Plan to achieve the stated objective and finally highlight the major risks which could undermine performance. These papers are consolidated into the Business Plan, together with the five-year financial forecasts and an overview written by the Airport Director. The Business Plans are prepared over a four-month period and are submitted in late Autumn. Each Plan is then reviewed by the Managing Director, changes made and finalised by January. At this stage they become the primary source of financial data for consolidation within the Corporate Plan itself.

12. It must be emphasised that under the revised process, the preparation of the budget and four-year financial forecasts take place integrally with the writing

of the Business Plans, such that the Business Plans provide the basis of any improvement in performance and the budgets are the financial implications of implementing the Plans.

The Corporate Plan

13. The Corporate Plan as a document draws on the Airport Business Plans and expands the process to cover items which are centrally determined or have relevance to more than one airport. The Corporate Plan represents the nucleus of BAA's forward planning. It is the mechanism by which the Board sanctions the overall objectives, policies and future strategies of the Authority. As such, the Corporate Plan will continue to be updated annually, and will normally come to the BAA Board for approval in March.

14. Prior to 1985, the Corporate Plan served two distinct purposes. Firstly it contained the objectives of the Authority and a series of policy statements on the various functions and responsibilities of the Authority. Policy statements were given, for example, on safety, security, capacity development, design, manpower, charging and consultation. These policies, although essential to the Plan itself, tend not to be subject to major alterations from year to year and create the framework within which planning takes place.

15. The second purpose of the Plan was to set out the strategies and forward forecasts of the Authority. This consisted of a review of the previous year, a statement about future traffic and economic assumptions, the preferred development strategy, the commercial strategy, the financial forecasts over five years and finally a range of sensitivities to test the robustness of the projections. These sections need to be re-written each year and in effect constitute the Plan for which Board approval is sought each year.

16. The Corporate Plan as presented this year is structured so as to more clearly recognise these two elements.

17. The Corporate Plan is presented to the Board for approval in March. Following approval, copies are given to the Department of Transport and are subsequently discussed between the Secretary of State and the BAA Board. These discussions are an important part of the Corporate Planning process, as they provide the opportunity to agree the overall strategic framework within which the Authority can then operate.

18. The Corporate Plan is used as a primary method of communicating not only with the Government but also with the employees, the unions and the airlines. The draft Corporate Plan is submitted to the unions in May for consultation purposes and a special meeting of the Joint Negotiating and Consultative Council is held at which the Corporate Plan is presented and discussed in detail. In June it is circulated to all senior BAA staff and made available to all employees. In mid-year the airlines and other air transport customers receive 'Policies and Programmes', based extensively on the Corporate Plan, as an information document for consultations. This document, too, forms the main item on detailed discussion with airlines in the Consultation Co-ordinating Council.

19. An important feature of BAA's Corporate Plan is the manner in which the process of producing it has become firmly interwoven with the entire management of the business. Thus:

—The financial forecasting has become an integral part of the planning system and the detailed one-year budget, prepared in January, is derived from the Business Plans.

—The Appraisal Papers, contained within the Business Plans, are written by line management and describe what each is intending to do and achieve over the next few years. They thus become part of an on-going management control system.

—The targets, agreed with Government and subsequently expanded throughout the Authority, are incorporated into the Business Plans and the Appraisal Papers, performance being monitored and reviewed on a monthly basis.

—Each Business Plan is formally approved and the financial and capital implications accepted by the Managing Director at the Review Meetings.

Summary

20. The principal stages in the development of the Authority's annual Corporate Plan are summarised in the following timetable, although it must be stressed that this is an evolving process subject to refinement each year.

May–June	—Board agreement to objectives, targets, policies and traffic forecasts
July	—Corporate Appraisal Meeting
August–November	—Airport Business Plans prepared
December–January	—Business Plans reviewed by Managing Director and consolidated within draft Corporate Plan
March	—Corporate Plan submitted to the Board
April–May	—Consultation with staff/unions/DTp
June	—Corporate Plan published
	—' Policies and Programmes' document sent to airlines

BAA Planning Department
March 1985

The development of airport commercial functions between 1983 and 1985

1. Heathrow

1.1. In response to the central proposals for the creation of the Trading Department Heathrow Management decided to abolish the Airport Commercial Department. Five commercial posts were retained or established at the airport.

1.2. The Catering Advisor and subordinate were retained and report to the Deputy Director Terminals.

1.3. A specialist Commercial post was established in each of the three existing Terminals but the reporting responsibility for these individuals was through a Property and Commercial Manager to the General Manager for the Terminal. The Property and Commercial Managers had previously carried Property Management functions only.

1.4. Terminal 4 will have a Commercial Manager covering both the Property and Commercial functions.

1.5. The Estates function at Heathrow has remained unchanged in scope or its reporting responsibility to the Deputy Director/Terminals. However, an internal reorganisation is under way to more closely integrate the professional Estates Surveyors and the Property Management functions.

2. Gatwick

2.1. A Commercial Manager post was established in 1983 which reports to the Property and Commercial Manager. The Catering Adviser and the Assistant Manager Commercial report to it.

2.2. The Estates Surveying and Property Management functions were integrated in 1983 and come under the control of a professionally qualified Estates Manager. The Estates Manager reports to the Property and Commercial Manager.

3. Scottish Airports

3.1. In 1985 a Commercial Manager post was established at Scottish Airports Head Office reporting to the Finance Manager.

3.2. At Prestwick the responsibility for the Commercial and Property functions lies with the Property and Commercial Manager.

3.3. At Glasgow the responsibility for the Commercial and Property functions lies with the Commercial and Finance Manager.

4. Stansted

4.1. In February 1985 a new post of Traffic and Commercial Manager was established which took responsibility for the existing Terminal Management and Public Relations functions including Airport marketing.

Source: **BAA.**

Property management

Statement for the Monopolies and Mergers Commission 28 June 1985

This note provides a brief summary of the history and current position on the BAA property management computer system. The system is in use at Gatwick and Stansted. Some aspects of Heathrow's needs are not yet provided and these are under discussion with Estates Management. Scottish Airports do not yet operate a computer based property management system though it is planned to examine their needs shortly.

1. *Start dates*
   —Initially a system was introduced at LHR in July 1976 based on the Honeywell level 66 mainframe with connection to intelligent programmable terminals (INCOTERMS).
   —A feasibility report in April 1981 recommended the development of a new system for Gatwick and Stansted. This would provide their needs in full while avoiding the technical difficulties at Heathrow associated with the growing obsolescence of the INCOTERM equipment. It was envisaged that Heathrow would, in due course, use the same system.
   —During the feasibility study a number of packages were examined but were discarded as unsuitable.
   —The outline system design produced in January 1982 included the requirements outlined by all three airports.
   —The new system was developed and went live as follows:
   Gatwick: Jan 84
   Heathrow: Apr 84
   Stansted: Nov 84.

2. *Objectives*
   —The original computer system replaced a manual ledger system. The new system was designed to cover some functions not included in the original system, to provide a flexible query and report system (via MDQS and later QRP) and to overcome the technical problems. The benefits were identified as avoidance of lost income and increased staff productivity to cope with an increasing workload.
   —System components included:
   Property schedules
   Company lists
   Agreements
   Meters.

3. Costs

The replacement system was estimated to cost £159,000 at January 1982 prices. Costs to end June 1985 are approximately £313,000. Concern over the continued escalation of these costs led to the decision to review the future of this project before proceeding further.

4. Achievements

—The system operates satisfactorily for Gatwick and Stansted.

—At Heathrow, although a computer based property management system has been operating for almost nine years, there are a number of user requirements which have not been met. These fall into four main categories:

(i) Detailed layout changes to reports or screens

(ii) Enhancements to the specification

(iii) Reports and screen displays not yet available

(iv) The ability to generate reports on an *ad hoc* basis using a report generator.

—Some of the missing reports are regarded by Heathrow as 'absolutely essential' and therefore the system will not be perceived as fully operational until this is remedied.

—Heathrow were also dissatisfied with the system response times, although recent improvements have removed this concern.

—The biggest stumbling block has been the lack of a report generator (item (iv) above). The intention to use the QRP language has been thwarted technically.

5. Environment

—Organisationally Heathrow is significantly more complex than Gatwick or Stansted. The lines of responsibility differ with some direct and some functional reporting relationships to the Estate Manager.

—The volume of property information is significantly higher at Heathrow.

—Data transfer from the old system at Heathrow caused problems which did not arise at Gatwick starting from a manual basis.

6. Progress on Review of System

—A review was started in January 1985 leading to a discussion document in March. Following discussion with Heathrow agreement was reached that a set of reports would be produced by *ad hoc* COBOL programs in order to overcome the inability to use the QRP language with the complex database design. The system would then be reviewed following a six months period of operation. Management Services would pay for these programs to be written by an external organisation in order to save time.

—Property Management produced detailed specifications of their needs during April and passed these to the Business Systems Manager for action.

—During May Business Systems assessed the work content and cost of the detailed requests. The costs and timescales were considered too great to proceed and a further set of meetings took place in an attempt to negotiate a reduction to acceptable levels by discussion with Heathrow Estates Management.

—Even after reducing to what Heathrow regarded as the ' absolutely essential ' requirements, the costs/timescales were considered unacceptable. At the last meeting held on 14 June, a full examination of the perceived options took place. The decisions reached were:

  (i) Honeywell be asked to re-examine the QRP difficulties and to recommend a suitable alternative if appropriate.

 (ii) Management Services to carry out a highly limited development of reports relating to the Property Ledger, subject to recalculation of costs and timescales.

(iii) Initiate an evaluation of package solutions to the overall requirements including the ability to generate *ad hoc* reports. Management Services will produce the terms of reference and pay for the study. The study will include the MENTOR system (used by British Rail), the WIMS package, and the Estate Computer Systems package (used by the CAA).

—Following the reports from Honeywell and from the package evaluations, a decision will be taken on the best way forward, whether package or in-house, in the light of the extra costs and benefits identified.

Source: BAA.

APPENDIX 6.2

(referred to in paragraph 6.20)

Current trading information systems

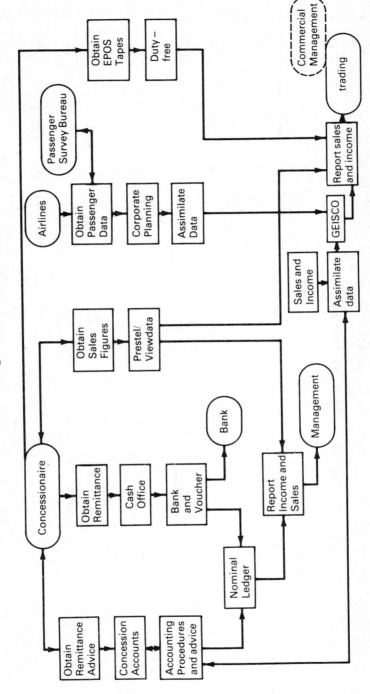

Source: BAA.

APPENDIX 7.1

(referred to in paragraphs 1.30 and 7.24)

BAA: budgets, out-turn and variances

£ million

	1980–81			1981–82			1982–83			1983–84			1984–85		
	Budget	Actual	Vari-ance	Budget	Actual	Vari-ance	Budget	Actual	Vari-ance	Budget	Actual	Vari-ance	Budget	Actual	Vari-ance
Income															
Landing fees	129·7	123·2	(6·5)	133·0	125·6	(7·4)	127·6	117·3	(10·3)	125·6	127·5	1·9	139·3	139·3	—
Aircraft parking fees	23·0	21·9	(1·1)	24·0	26·3	2·3	26·3	25·7	(0·6)	28·8	28·2	(0·6)	29·7	30·1	0·4
Apron and other services	6·5	6·5	—	7·2	7·6	0·4	8·3	8·4	0·1	10·3	10·4	0·1	11·9	12·4	0·5
Trading concessions	65·1	65·0	(0·1)	68·9	74·0	5·1	79·5	85·0	5·5	91·6	98·7	7·1	112·2	118·8	6·6
Rents and services	34·7	36·0	1·3	41·5	42·2	0·7	47·2	46·4	(0·8)	49·9	50·1	0·2	56·9	59·9	3·0
Miscellaneous income	1·2	1·1	(0·1)	1·3	1·1	(0·2)	1·3	1·1	(0·2)	1·6	1·9	0·3	1·7	1·8	0·1
Total income	260·2	253·7	(6·5)	275·9	276·8	0·9	290·2	283·9	(6·3)	307·8	316·8	9·0	351·7	362·3	10·6
Expenditure															
Staff costs	82·3	79·5	2·8	89·7	84·4	5·3	91·2	89·7	1·5	92·8	92·8	—	100·5	99·6	0·9
Rent, rates	13·1	12·5	0·6	16·4	16·8	(0·4)	18·6	18·2	0·4	20·4	19·2	1·2	22·3	20·0	2·3
Utility services	25·7	25·6	0·1	30·9	29·4	1·5	31·3	31·7	(0·4)	33·5	33·2	0·3	35·3	36·0	(0·7)
Equipment and supplies	6·6	5·9	0·7	7·4	7·7	(0·3)	7·9	8·3	(0·4)	8·6	9·6	(1·0)	9·2	12·2	(3·0)
Maintenance and repairs	16·5	14·8	1·7	17·2	17·1	0·1	20·1	18·4	1·7	20·4	19·6	0·8	18·9	18·6	0·3
Other expenses	29·8	31·3	(1·5)	30·0	30·7	(0·7)	29·2	25·4	3·8	30·6	30·9	(0·3)	30·5	34·1	(3·6)
Labour and material capitalised	(4·0)	(4·9)	0·9	(5·2)	(5·1)	(0·1)	(5·3)	(4·8)	(0·5)	(5·6)	(6·0)	0·4	(6·2)	(6·4)	0·2
Depreciation	61·3	51·4	9·9	59·6	57·3	2·3	68·6	65·2	3·4	70·0	67·9	2·1	80·3	76·2	4·1
Total expenditure	231·3	216·1	15·2	246·0	238·3	7·7	261·6	252·1	9·5	270·7	267·2	3·5	290·8	290·3	0·5
CCA trading profit	28·9	37·6	8·7	29·9	38·5	8·6	28·6	31·8	3·2	37·1	49·6	12·5	60·9	72·0	11·1
Prior year adjustments etc		0·3			1·2			3·2			2·0			—	
CCA trading profit as per statutory accs		37·9			39·7			35·0			51·6			72·0	

Source: BAA.

Note: Reasons for differences between the above figures and those in Table 7.1 and in other appendices include, first, the additional depreciation referred to in the note to Table 7.1 and, secondly, the split of prior year adjustments between income and expenditure, together with some netting between categories. The latter covers such items as promotional schemes with concessionaires, repayments works services for tenants and miscellaneous income accruing to Head Office.

APPENDIX 7.2

(referred to in paragraph 7.49)

BAA: commercial contributions to non-controllable costs and profits

£'000

	Total	Total Concessions	Duty-free liquor	Other duty- & tax-free	Tax-paid	Catering	Advertising	Car hire	Parking	Other concessions	Advertising administered by concessionaires	Rents & services	Misc
Year ended 31 March 1984													
Income	149,309	98,847	22,056	34,538	8,534	5,301	1,307	4,203	13,928	8,980	—	49,877	585
Controllable costs													
Staff costs	125	—	—	—	—	—	—	—	—	—	—	125	—
Management fees	2,050	2,050	—	—	—	—	—	—	2,050	—	—	—	—
Rent and rates	4,523	2,868	205	172	223	946	135	188	885	114	—	1,655	—
Cleaning	930	302	8	6	10	126	—	2	140	10	—	628	—
Maintenance	8,178	3,668	215	156	215	1,881	32	11	1,077	81	—	4,510	—
Services	22,399	795	127	66	64	326	—	3	168	41	—	21,604	—
Depreciation	11,141	3,894	298	244	288	1,553	4	50	1,302	155	—	7,247	—
Miscellaneous	287	332	95	94	21	(4)	125	1	—	—	—	(45)	—
Total controllable costs	49,633	13,909	948	738	821	4,828	296	255	5,622	401	—	35,724	—
Contribution to non-controllable costs and profit	99,676	84,938	21,108	33,800	7,713	473	1,011	3,948	8,306	8,579	—	14,153	585
Year ended 31 March 1985													
Income	178,951	118,866	25,578	43,498	10,140	6,255	1,931	5,151	16,312	10,988	(987)	59,312	773
Controllable costs													
Staff costs	124	—	—	—	—	—	—	—	—	—	—	124	—
Management fees	2,199	2,199	—	—	—	—	—	—	2,199	—	—	—	—
Rent and rates	4,672	3,072	215	182	271	971	77	319	915	122	—	1,600	—
Cleaning	960	318	8	5	8	130	—	2	155	10	—	642	—
Maintenance	9,414	3,860	213	146	274	1,727	34	30	1,391	45	—	5,554	—
Services	25,548	1,049	171	92	66	421	—	3	275	21	—	24,499	—
Depreciation	12,413	4,668	338	401	352	1,893	15	59	1,517	93	—	7,745	—
Miscellaneous	301	477	120	120	—	—	237	—	—	—	—	(176)	—
Total controllable costs	55,631	15,643	1,065	946	971	5,142	363	413	6,452	291	—	39,988	—
Contribution to non-controllable costs and profit	123,320	103,223	24,513	42,552	9,169	1,113	1,568	4,738	9,860	10,697	(987)	19,324	773

Source: MMC from BAA data.

Note: Controllable costs include direct costs and indirect costs to the extent that they are controllable by local management and chargeable to specific activities. Other indirect costs and general overhead expenses are treated as non-controllable costs.

3162890

L

APPENDIX 7.3
(referred to in paragraph 7.49)

Commercial activities: current cost income and expenditure by airport

	1980–81 £'000	1981–82 £'000	1982–83 £'000	1983–84 £'000	1984–85 £'000	Increase/ (decrease) 1980–81 to 1984–85 %
Heathrow						
Income						
Duty-free liquor						
Duty-free tobacco						
Other tax-free						
Tax-paid						
Catering		[*Figures omitted. See note on page iv.*]				
Advertising						
Car hire						
Parking						
Other concession income						
Advertising administered by concessionaires	—	—	—	—	[*]	N/A
Total concession income	43,770	48,489	54,515	61,737	73,929	68·9
Rents and services		[*Figures omitted. See note on page iv.*]				
Miscellaneous						
Total commercial income	70,511	79,130	88,430	98,191	118,303	67·8
Expenditure						
Direct costs		[*Figures omitted. See note on page iv.*]				
Indirect costs						
Overhead allocations						
Total expenditure	41,854	46,733	47,711	49,460	57,794	38·1
Current cost commercial trading profit	28,657	32,397	40,719	48,731	60,509	111·1
Commercial trading profit as a percentage of total commercial income	40·6	40·9	46·0	49·6	51·1	

* Figures omitted. See note on page iv.

158

	1980–81	1981–82	1982–83	1983–84	1984–85	Increase/ (decrease) 1980–81 to 1984–85
	£'000	£'000	£'000	£'000	£'000	%

Gatwick

Income

Duty-free liquor						
Duty-free tobacco						
Other tax-free						
Tax-paid						
Catering		[*Figures omitted.*				
Advertising		*See note on page iv.*]				
Car hire						
Parking						
Other concession income						
Advertising administered by concessionaires	—	—	—	—	[*]	N/A
Total concession income	15,669	19,231	22,441	28,545	34,785	122.0
Rents and services		[*Figures omitted. See note on page iv.*]				
Miscellaneous						
Total commercial income	20,929	25,861	30,023	36,890	44,278	111.6

Expenditure

Direct costs						
Indirect costs		[*Figures omitted.*				
Overhead allocations		*See note on page iv.*]				
Total expenditure	10,429	12,048	12,215	14,348	16,915	62.2
Current cost commercial trading profit	10,500	13,813	17,808	22,542	27,363	160.6
Commercial trading profit as a percentage of total commercial income	50.2	53.4	59.3	61.1	61.8	

* Figures omitted. See note on page iv.

	1980–81	1981–82	1982–83	1983–84	1984–85	Increase/ (decrease) 1980–81 to 1984–85
	£'000	£'000	£'000	£'000	£'000	%

Stansted

Income
Duty-free liquor
Duty-free tobacco
Other tax-free
Tax-paid
Catering
Advertising
Car hire
Parking
Other concession income

[Figures omitted. See note on page iv.]

	1980–81	1981–82	1982–83	1983–84	1984–85	%
Total concession income	570	653	771	945	1,294	127·0

Rents and services
Miscellaneous

[Figures omitted. See note on page iv.]

	1980–81	1981–82	1982–83	1983–84	1984–85	%
Total commercial income	1,319	1,604	1,650	1,895	2,351	78·2

Expenditure
Direct costs
Indirect costs
Overhead allocations

[Figures omitted. See note on page iv.]

	1980–81	1981–82	1982–83	1983–84	1984–85	%
Total expenditure	1,811	2,611	1,873	1,397	1,399	(22·7)
Current cost commercial trading profit	(492)	(1,007)	(223)	498	952	N/A
Commercial trading profit as a percentage of total commercial income	—	—	—	26.3	40·5	

160

	1980–81	1981–82	1982–83	1983–84	1984–85	Increase/ (decrease) 1980–81 to 1984–85
	£'000	£'000	£'000	£'000	£'000	%

Glasgow

Income
Duty-free liquor
Duty-free tobacco
Other tax-free
Tax-paid
Catering
Advertising
Car hire
Parking
Other concession income

[*Figures omitted.
See note on page iv.*]

	1980–81	1981–82	1982–83	1983–84	1984–85	%
Total concession income	2,592	2,978	3,401	3,797	4,569	76·3

Rents and services
Miscellaneous

[*Figures omitted. See note on page iv.*]

	1980–81	1981–82	1982–83	1983–84	1984–85	%
Total commercial income	3,418	4,210	4,734	5,164	6,174	80·6

Expenditure
Direct costs
Indirect costs
Overhead allocations

[*Figures omitted.
See note on page iv.*]

	1980–81	1981–82	1982–83	1983–84	1984–85	%
Total expenditure	1,450	1,901	2,036	2,067	2,340	61·4
Current cost commercial trading profit	1,968	2,309	2,698	3,097	3,834	94·8
Commercial trading profit as a percentage of total commercial income	57·6	54·8	57·0	60·0	62·1	

	1980–81	1981–82	1982–83	1983–84	1984–85	Increase/ (decrease) 1980–81 to 1984–85
	£'000	£'000	£'000	£'000	£'000	%

Edinburgh

Income
  Duty-free liquor
  Duty-free tobacco
  Other tax-free
  Tax-paid
  Catering
  Advertising
  Car hire
  Parking
  Other concession
    income

[*Figures omitted.*
See note on page iv.]

	1980–81	1981–82	1982–83	1983–84	1984–85	%
Total concession income	977	1,162	1,300	1,627	1,935	98·1

Rents and
  services
Miscellaneous

[*Figures omitted.   See note on page iv.*]

	1980–81	1981–82	1982–83	1983–84	1984–85	%
Total commercial income	1,424	1,666	1,933	2,301	2,687	88·7

Expenditure
  Direct costs
  Indirect costs
  Overhead
    allocations

[*Figures omitted.*
See note on page iv.]

	1980–81	1981–82	1982–83	1983–84	1984–85	%
Total expenditure	1,301	1,527	1,393	1,416	1,416	8·8
Current cost commercial trading profit	123	139	540	885	1,271	933·3
Commercial trading profit as a percentage of total commercial income	8·6	8·3	27·9	38·5	47·3	

	1980–81	1981–82	1982–83	1983–84	1984–85	Increase/ (decrease) 1980–81 to 1984–85
	£'000	£'000	£'000	£'000	£'000	%

Prestwick

Income
Duty-free liquor
Duty-free tobacco
Other tax-free
Tax-paid
Catering
Advertising
Car hire
Parking
Other concession income

[*Figures omitted. See note on page iv.*]

	1980–81	1981–82	1982–83	1983–84	1984–85	%
Total concession income	961	901	718	775	860	(10·5)

Rents and services
Miscellaneous

[*Figures omitted. See note on page iv.*]

Total commercial income	2,109	2,241	1,928	2,022	2,171	2·9

Expenditure
Direct costs
Indirect costs
Overhead allocations

[*Figures omitted. See note on page iv.*]

Total expenditure	1,616	1,806	1,495	1,534	1,327	(17·9)
Current cost commercial trading profit	493	435	433	488	844	71·2
Commercial trading profit as a percentage of total commercial income	23·4	19·4	22·5	24·1	38·9	

	1980–81	1981–82	1982–83	1983–84	1984–85	Increase/ (decrease) 1980–81 to 1984–85
	£'000	£'000	£'000	£'000	£'000	%

Aberdeen

Income
  Duty-free liquor
  Duty-free tobacco
  Other tax-free
  Tax-paid
  Catering
  Advertising
  Car hire
  Parking
  Other concession
    income

[*Figures omitted.*
See note on page iv.]

	1980–81	1981–82	1982–83	1983–84	1984–85	%
Total concession income	772	980	1,180	1,422	1,494	93·5

Rents and
  services
Miscellaneous

[*Figures omitted.   See note on page iv.*]

	1980–81	1981–82	1982–83	1983–84	1984–85	%
Total commercial income	1,998	2,350	2,518	2,847	2,987	49·5

Expenditure
  Direct costs
  Indirect costs
  Overhead
    allocations

[*Figures omitted.*
See note on page iv.]

	1980–81	1981–82	1982–83	1983–84	1984–85	%
Total expenditure	1,315	1,435	1,356	1,383	1,467	11·6
Current cost commercial trading profit	683	915	1,162	1,464	1,520	122·5
Commercial trading profit as a percentage of total commercial income	34·2	38·9	46·1	51·4	50·9	

Source: BAA.

APPENDIX 7.4

(referred to in paragraph 7.49)

Commercial activities: CCA return on capital employed

	1982–83			1983–84			1984–85		
	Average capital employed £'000	Net profit/ (loss) £'000	Return %	Average capital employed £'000	Net profit £'000	Return %	Average capital employed £'000	Net profit £'000	Return %
Heathrow	99,895	40,719	40·8	99,001	48,731	49·2	106,015	60,509	57·1
Gatwick	58,491	17,808	30·4	60,200	22,542	37·4	60,461	27,363	45·3
Stansted	5,897	(223)	(3·8)	5,145	498	9·7	5,664	952	16·8
Glasgow	5,228	2,698	51·6	4,899	3,097	63·2	5,180	3,834	74·0
Edinburgh	4,218	540	12·8	3,998	885	22·1	4,496	1,272	28·3
Prestwick	4,249	433	10·2	4,460	488	10·9	3,343	845	25·3
Aberdeen	3,719	1,162	31·2	4,594	1,464	31·9	4,585	1,520	33·2
Total all airports	181,697	63,137	35·0	182,297	77,705	42·6	189,744	96,295	50·7

Source: MMC from BAA data.

Note: The figures shown for average capital employed do not include an allocation of the assets in use by utility services, airport common services, or Head Office. Assets in course of construction are likewise excluded.

(referred to in paragraph 12.5)

BAA manpower plan

BAA staff

	1985–86	1986–87	1987–88	1988–89	1989–90	
Total	7,477	7,672	7,886	7,928	7,992	
Trainees	174	183	184	186	186	
HO	739	765	781	788	792	
Scotland	1,329	1,333	1,334	1,337	1,338	
Stansted	186	191	196	206	216	
Gatwick	1,301	1,332	1,533	1,573	1,622	
Heathrow	3,748	3,868	3,858	3,838	3,838	

YEAR

Source: BAA.

166

Pay for non-industrial employees (1.1.85 rates)

Note: The minima of all the scales and ranges relate to employees aged 20 or over

£ per annum

Scale paid bands

Band 9	Band 8	Band 7
5,103 (× 153)	5,565 (× 159)	6,135 (× 186)
5,256	5,724	6,321
5,409	5,883	6,507
5,562	6,042	6,693
5,715	6,201	6,879
5,868	6,360	7,065

Band 6	Band 5	Band 4
6,738 (× 204)	7,635 (× 243)	8,829 (× 273)
6,942	7,878	9,102
7,146	8,121	9,375
7,350	8,364	9,648
7,554	8,607	9,921
7,758	8,850	10,194
7,962	9,093	10,467

Range paid bands

	Minimum	*Maximum*
Band 3	10,137 (× 312)	12,321
Band 2	11,853 (× 417)	14,772
Band 1	14,400 (× 516)	18,012

Source: BAA.

(referred to in paragraphs 1.75 and 12.14)

Joint negotiating and consultative machinery

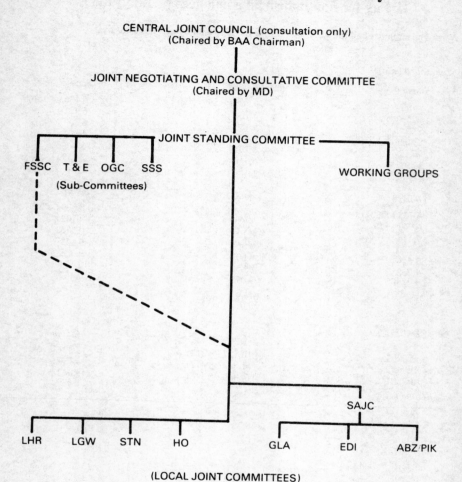

CENTRAL JOINT COUNCIL (consultation only)
(Chaired by BAA Chairman)

JOINT NEGOTIATING AND CONSULTATIVE COMMITTEE
(Chaired by MD)

JOINT STANDING COMMITTEE

FSSC   T & E   OGC   SSS
(Sub-Committees)

WORKING GROUPS

SAJC

LHR   LGW   STN   HO   GLA   EDI   ABZ/PIK

(LOCAL JOINT COMMITTEES)

FSSC = Fire Service Sub-Committee

T & E = Training & Education Sub-Committee

OGC = Operative Grading Committee

SSS = Superannuation Sub-Committee

SAJC = Scottish Airports Joint Committee

Source: **BAA.**

168

APPENDIX 12.4

(referred to in paragraph 12.14)

Heathrow airport negotiating and consultative machinery

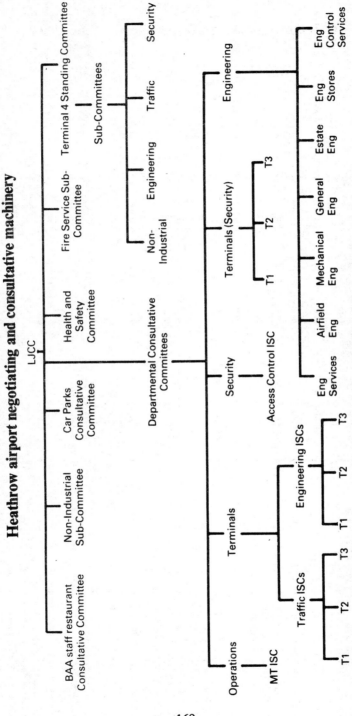

Note: ISC = Industrial Sub-Committee.

Source: BAA.

APPENDIX 13.1
(referred to in paragraph 13.5)

Summary of passenger service standards

January 1985

Facility	Waiting time % of passengers within a stated time	Space for passengers waiting up to	Personal space per person — standing	Personal space per person — sitting	Seating for % of people present
Check-in	95% up to 3 minutes	10 mins	—	—	—
Departures concourse			0·8m²	1·0m²	10%
*Passenger search and Passport control	1st process: 95% up to 3 mins	5 mins	1·0m²	—	—
	2nd process: 95% up to 1 min	1 min	0·6m²	—	—
Departures lounge		—	1·0m²	1·0m²	60%
*Satellites, Gaterooms		—	1·0m²	1·0m²	60%
Gaterooms		—	1·0m²	0·8m²	70%
*Immigration: UK/EEC	95% up to 4 mins	12 mins	1·0m²		
: others	95% up to 12 mins	30 mins	0·6m²		
*Buffer Hall	Max 25 mins from 1st passenger out of immigration to last bag on unit	—	1·0m²	0·8m²	40%
*Baggage reclaim			0·6m²†		5%
Arrivals concourse		—	1·0m²	0·8m²	20%
Lifts	95% up to 2 mins	—			
	50% up to 0·5 mins	—			

* = Revised/extended standards

† = trolley effects to be added

Other standards
Forecourts: 95% chance of finding a space.
Piers: Walking distances: max 250m unaided.
    max 650m with walkway (of which 200m max unaided).
    rapid transit for point-to-point journeys over 500m.

Pier service (with loading bridge) for at least 75–80% of passengers.
Source: BAA.

Printed by Her Majesty's Stationery Office
Dd 601644   12/85   C17 3162890